D1446807

How Talking Cures

Dialog-on-Freud Series
Series Editor: M. Andrew Holowchak

The Dialog-on-Freud series invites authors to explore the history and practice of analytic therapies through critical analysis of and expatiation on the seminal work of Freud. It seeks books that critically scrutinize the numerous facets of Freud's work over the course of his life, that investigate how or to what extent Freud's thinking causally gave rise to the various sorts of therapies that currently exist, and that examine the relevance of Freud's thinking today for those therapies.

Titles in the series

How Talking Cures

Revealing Freud's Contributions to All Psychotherapies

Lee Jaffe

ROWMAN & LITTLEFIELD
Lanham • Boulder • New York • London

Published by Rowman & Littlefield
A wholly owned subsidiary of The Rowman & Littlefield Publishing Group, Inc.
4501 Forbes Boulevard, Suite 200, Lanham, Maryland 20706
www.rowman.com

16 Carlisle Street, London W1D 3BT, United Kingdom

British Library Cataloguing in Publication Information Available

Library of Congress Cataloging-in-Publication Data

Library of Congress Cataloging-in-Publication Data Available
ISBN 978-1-4422-3989-0 (cloth : alk. paper) -- ISBN 978-1-4422-3990-6 (electronic)

∞ ™ The paper used in this publication meets the minimum requirements of American National Standard for Information Sciences Permanence of Paper for Printed Library Materials, ANSI/NISO Z39.48-1992.

Printed in the United States of America

Contents

Preface

While the title of this book refers to "talking cures," in this instance the word "cure" is not used in the strict medical sense as it applies to the elimination of diseases or the physical repair of damage to the body. Instead, it is used to refer to psychotherapeutic interventions that reduce psychologically based suffering and psychopathological dysfunctionality. Mental and emotional conflicts, unlike a typical medical disease, are normal to mental life and cannot be eliminated. Mental health is about flexibility and finding successful adaptations that minimize pain, that maximize pleasure, and that permit an adaptation that fits within the demands of external reality.

Furthermore, the term "talking cures" does not only refer to talking. There are many non-verbal aspects of the treatment and actions taken by provider and/or the patient that will be part of the treatment. For example, when treatment is face-to-face there is an exchange of non-verbal looks and tone of voice. Sometimes the patient may reach out to shake hands, and at times a patient might even pursue a hug. While there are and clearly should be boundaries that limit physical contact, and there is no therapeutic defense for sexual boundary violations, there can be a space for some touching that will hold other meanings. What does it mean, for example, if on a first meeting a patient reaches out to shake hands and is refused? Also, there can be actions that take the form of being late or early, or of forgetting sessions. While this merely names a few, the point is to appreciate that "talking cures" does not and cannot be reduced to the content of what is spoken.

The inspiration and impetus for this book comes from teaching seminars on Freud to psychiatric residents and other students in psychotherapy training. Unlike the students in our psychoanalytic institutes, who read Freud and get exposure to his thinking, the students and clinicians I encounter outside of analytic institutes often have little or no direct exposure to the knowledge and the practical application of Freud's body of work. Moreover, the contemporary approaches to psychotherapy they have learned, unlike Freud's, do not anchor an understanding of psychopathology in an understanding of how the normal mind works; most notably that the human mind is always a mind-in-conflict, such that abnormal psychology is understood as the maladaptive management of a mind-in-conflict and external reality. These students frequently come to seminars on Freud with at best an uneducated curiosity about his work, sometimes with an uninformed dismissal of his work, but at worst they have already adopted an ignorant attitude of disdain and contempt.

Suffice it to say; teaching such non-psychoanalytically oriented residents, students and clinicians is challenging. Early on I learned that I had to find ways to relate Freud's ideas to theories that were familiar to these students, and to directly apply these concepts to the patients they were responsible for treating; patients who frequently were not appropriate for psychoanalytic treatment. In other words, I had to find ways to make Freud clear and relevant to the treatment of patients who were psychotic, who suffered from debilitating addictions, who had severe personality disorders, who were in highly dysfunctional relationships, to couples, as well as understanding those patients who were more psychologically intact and capable of higher functioning. So my students' ears perked up, for example, when I told them Freud came up with versions of supportive psychotherapy, cognitive-behavioral therapy, and expressive psychotherapy more than a century ago.

As I cultivated these seminars over the years, with the help of my students, I developed a perspective on Freud's work that identified six modalities of therapeutic action, some that Freud described explicitly, and others that I found implicit in the different stages of his thinking. During each presentation and lecture of these therapeutic actions, students are invited to discuss their patients, both so we can explore how these six therapeutic actions work, and so we can identify which ones are indicated or contra-indicated for each patient and why. After teaching the seminar a number of times, I noticed that some students always asked me for references that would elaborate on these ideas. They told me that they were surprised to find Freud so useful and practical, and asked me if I had written about these ideas, or was there an article or book I could recommend? So in the end, this book is written in response to my students.

It is important to keep in mind that while I define six different modalities of therapeutic action, and in some places I will also describe actual clinical interventions as well, no book can substitute for clinical supervision in learning the technique of any form of psychotherapy or psychoanalysis with actual patients. One of the major problems with the current trend to "manualize" psychotherapies is the assumption that the patient's individuality need not be considered. But people are not like cars, where a manual can describe how to do each procedure on a particular automobile, based on the fact that they are built alike; and even with cars there have to be different manuals for different cars. But with humans, like our fingerprints, our voices, our faces, our minds are far more individualized than models and makes of automobiles. For this reason, in psychotherapy, what one anxious patient may experience as therapeutic support and concern, another might experience as intrusive and threatening.

Furthermore, the manualized oversimplification of the psychotherapeutic encounter, unable to take account of the fact that the psychotherapy relationship is co-constructed, seems like a giant step backward to the days in psychoanalysis when it was believed that the abstinent psychoanalyst should adhere to the maxim, "Don't do something; just stand there." This approach was based on the mistaken belief in a "one-person psychology," the idea that the therapist's actions or inactions can be independent of the patient's subjective experience of reality and vice versa. I find it ironic that while psychoanalysis has largely outgrown this oversimplification of human experience, in favor of what is often referred to as a "two-person psychology," many modern approaches to psychotherapy seem to be taking a giant step backward, in part to serve the needs of traditional research that require the comparison of uniform groups. But can it possibly be that patients have the same experience of a manualized treatment approach?

So you will not find in this book a manual defining specifically how and when to employ the therapeutic actions in a unified and systematic system of psychotherapy. Instead, in implementing these six modalities of therapeutic action, it will be essential to consider the patient's personality; moreover, it is important to consider the therapist's personality, and the interaction between the two. All therapists will find it easier to work with some of these therapeutic actions than others, as will all patients. It is in part for this reason that psychoanalytic training requires the candidate-in-training undergo a personal analysis, and even then it is understood that no one can become the ideal analyst who has equal comfort and ability to access the full range of interventions that might be in the best interest of the patient at different points in a treatment. Still, with these individualized considerations and limitations in mind, knowledge of the six modes of therapeutic action is essential in determining what approaches to consider, even though the clinical decision process in any particular case cannot be formulaic, and the therapist may find some interventions challenging to execute successfully.

For the sake of simplicity and for the purposes of this book, I will use the term "therapist" inclusively to refer to all providers of talking cures, including psychoanalysts, psychoanalytic psychotherapists, cognitive-behavioral therapists, behavioral therapists, gestalt psychotherapists, therapists who treat couples, etc. I also use the term therapist to refer to all providers to reflect the fact that this book is about generic modes of psychotherapeutic action that are applicable to all talking cures. Again, keep in mind that a main point of this book is to elucidate the contemporary relevance of Freud's thinking to all forms of psychotherapy, and hopefully to show the pointlessness of participating in any form of competition over which talking cures are superior to others.

What comes to mind is an epigram, to the best of my recollection one that occurred to me during my undergraduate training in psychology and philosophy. It goes something like "The behaviorists are so Locke'd in that they Kant understand conditioning is not our only salivation." I recall at the time being caught up in all the competition between psychological theories and treatments. Were the behaviorists right to assume we are born a clean slate upon which our experiences are written, or were the psychoanalysts right to assume we are driven by unconscious forces that exist from birth? Being at an educational, undergraduate institution at a time when psychoanalytic thinking was favored over behaviorism, I became identified with one side against the other. Ironically, I was to find out that Freud was less committed to some of his specific ideas than I had become. It is my hope that by the end of this book you will also be convinced, as I have become convinced, that such allegiances are misguided and tend to limit an appreciation for the breadth and complexity of Freud's thinking, including the six basic forms of therapeutic action delineated in this book from his life's work.

Unfortunately, no book like this one could ever hope to credit everyone I have read who has contributed to developments in the field of mental health, so I apologize in advance to all those not cited, whose ideas have influenced my thinking. In fact, while I have certainly not read them all, this list of references could include everyone who has written about psychotherapy or psychoanalysis; all their contributions can be related to the six basic modes of therapeutic action that I have extracted from Freud's life's work. I do specifically reference some authors who have contributed to the more recent literature on therapeutic action, I cite some specific passages of Freud where necessary to support my definitions of the therapeutic actions, and I cite the authors I quote in a section deconstructing and comparing different views of the process of psychoanalysis.

Most of the credit, however, belongs to my teachers, my analyst, my mentors, and my colleagues, to all those at the San Diego Psychoanalytic Center, at the American Psychoanalytic Association, at the International Psychoanalytic Studies Organization, and at the International Psychoanalytical Association, who continue to reveal Freud's thinking to me. While it is not widely known, for the most part those who train psychoanalysts and psychoanalytic psychotherapists do it as a labor of love and dedication, by teaching on a voluntary basis, or taking reduced fees for supervision and the analysis of psychoanalysts-in-training.

More personally, I want to thank my dear friends and colleagues Robert and Phyllis Tyson, who suggested that this project was appropriate to a book format rather than an article in a professional journal, and who then directed me to a contact at Jason Aronson. I am most appreciative of my teacher and colleague, Alan Sugarman, who carefully read through an earlier version of the manuscript and made a number of helpful observations, as I am to the editors at Aronson who also made many helpful suggestions. Last but not least, I want to thank my wife, Susan, and my children, Kate and Megan, who have continued to support, nudge, and abide my labored efforts to write.

I believe it is also important to acknowledge that the analysis of Freud's work expressed in this book is mine, and will not be shared by everyone in the mental health field, much less by all psychoanalysts. Freud himself did not delineate these six modes of therapeutic action as I have done here, and there is considerable theoretical pluralism among providers of psychotherapy and psychoanalysis. Regrettably, this diversity of theories and treatment modalities has led to a Balkanization of talking cures with tribal, and at times even fanatical, battles (like the personal allegiances that I referred to earlier), both between psychoanalytic and non-psychoanalytic approaches, as well as within different psychoanalytic approaches.

But in fact, how many ways can there really be that one person talking with another or with a couple about their relationship brings about a cure? Surely, not as many ways as there are theories. What we need is an integrative model of cure and treatment, a way to deconstruct the essential elements of the healing processes that are accomplished by the relationship and words between therapist and patient, no matter what the general theory. Only in this way can we be clear about how the many different approaches to psychotherapy and psychoanalysis compare, and thereby determine which approach to recommend to a particular patient. The alternative is that treatment recommendations will be based on what the provider does, rather than what is in the best interest of a given patient. This book is an effort to delineate such a common ground by extracting from Freud's body of work six generic modes of psychotherapeutic action. So in the end, it is Freud himself who deserves the greatest acknowledgment.

But in order to acknowledge Freud's contributions, it is crucial to begin with an introduction to some basic background knowledge of how he worked, the history of talking cures that came before him, why he himself did not delineate these distinct generic modes of psychotherapeutic action from his own work, and why the valuable contributions of psychoanalysis have become so marginalized in the contemporary fields of psychiatry, psychology and the other allied mental health professions. What happened and why?

ONE

Introduction

Psychotherapeutic action refers to the mechanism(s) by which talking can have the potential to cure, like the expression of emotion or seeing something in a new way. References to psychotherapy, the *talking cures,* first appear in artifacts of ancient times. One of the earliest records of medical knowledge, the Egyptian Ebers Papyrus (1550 BCE), describes depression along with the power of magic (a form of suggestion by shamans) to influence human distress. While it is impossible to know how these ideas were actually used, they clearly did exist many, many centuries ago. In fact, throughout recorded history there is evidence of efforts to understand and alleviate human suffering that were based on talking. Thus, speech is a way to connect, to communicate, to feel, and to understand. Talking means talking with another person, making the relationship an essential aspect of the cure. One of the reasons psychoanalysis has such potential power to cure is that the frequency of sessions, up to four to five a week, and the longer duration of the treatment foster a deep connection between the patient and the analyst.

Now leap ahead in time over three thousand years. Sigmund Freud and his students of psychoanalysis stand out because they go beyond specific concepts of psychological suffering, beyond ideas about mental illness, to realize a unity of the human mind and a continuum of mental functioning from normal to pathological. From the initial years of Freud's work, it took less than one hundred years to see an explosion of different approaches to psychotherapy. Psychology is no longer only a way to understand what goes wrong and why, but also how to understand everyone's daily and nightly (i.e., dreaming) mental life. Conflict is no longer just about problems, but a normal feature of human nature, in part because civilization requires us to be *civilized animals;* societies impose restrictions on human behavior. Civilization is not possible if we all act on

1

'lict and desire. Dogs, for example, are free to forni-
>never they wish, whereas we, as civilized hu-
ᴜn our sexual desires, nor can we act freely on our
ᴜ; so our minds must be capable of controlling such

ᴜ do our atavistic, animal urges go? It was with Freud's later
.es, including the idea of a System Ucs (his label for the uncon-
.ᴜ as a system in the mind) that the unconscious was no longer just a
.ᴜderground place in the mind for hiding traumas, but an essential part
of normal mental functioning. Think of it; how could you ever master
driving an automobile or tying your shoes if you needed to think each
step of the procedures through every time, in the same way you did the
first time? Fortunately, such procedures develop into skills that become
learned, automatic, and unconscious. The ego psychologists called this
mental function "secondary automization." Nowadays the neuropsychol-
ogists call it procedural memory. It appears that a number of psychoanalytic concepts pre-date contemporary neuropsychological concepts by fif-
ty years, yet the mental functions they describe are essentially the same:
But how many psychoanalytic concepts have been lost or replaced by
new terminologies without acknowledgment?

My training as a child, adolescent, and adult psychoanalyst entailed a
very comprehensive, thorough study of psychoanalysis. The inspiration
for this book comes from those personal encounters with the substance
and significance of Sigmund Freud's ideas about who we are, how we
work, and how we can help people who are lost and suffering emotionally. I am startled by the disparity between the value of Freud's contributions and the present-day dismissal and disregard of the importance of
his ideas. The mental health professions are losing a great legacy and
resource for understanding how all psychotherapies work. Are Freud's
contributions really obsolete? Ask yourself, would Freud seem out of
date if you knew that one of his earliest theories was essentially the
theory of cognitive-behavioral psychotherapy? This is but one instance of
Freud's lost legacy, and this book is an effort to reclaim his many contributions to understanding how those who suffer emotionally can be
helped: *How talking cures.*

The truth is that Freud made numerous contributions to psychology
during a period from the late 1800s into the 1900s. In these prolific writings he endeavored to understand mental suffering, the human mind, the
relationship between the body and the mind, human nature, literature,
art, humor, history, and civilization itself. Through dreams and other
mental phenomena he discovered the ways of the unconscious: the rules
of condensation, displacement, symbolism, and timelessness among others, that permit us to make meaning of the world of the unconscious. He
helped us understand that psychosis and schizophrenia are not unique
states of mind, but disorders wherein the mechanisms that govern the

unconscious intrude into conscious thinking; in other words, when we dream we are in effect all functioning on a psychotic level.

Throughout his professional years Freud also created a succession of theories of psychopathology linked to methods of treatment. With the creation of psychoanalysis—in its heyday a radical and innovative treatment—mental health providers, mostly psychiatrists at first, learned and applied the new procedures to their patients suffering with various forms of mental illness, in some cases even including the more severe psychoses. Early on, psychoanalysis became so accepted and popular that the official psychiatric, diagnostic classification system was eventually based on its theories.

For the first three quarters of the twentieth century psychoanalysts continued to expand on psychoanalytic theories and treatments. During these years, psychoanalysts were among the leaders of medical schools, designing the programs for training psychiatrists. Psychiatric hospitals based their in-patient treatments on psychoanalytic principles. Academia embraced psychoanalysis in departments of art, the classics, economics, English, history, philosophy, political science, psychology, sociology, theater, and theology. Many private practitioners provided psychoanalytic treatments. In short, Freud's new science remapped the human mind. His ideas were so groundbreaking that he has been compared to pioneers like Copernicus, who remapped the universe, and Darwin, who remapped the origin of our species.

So why, at the beginning of the twenty-first century, has psychoanalysis lost so much of its prominence? What happened? How can it be possible that such momentous contributions to science are now commonly viewed as obsolete? Why the decline in the acceptance and popularity of psychoanalytic points of view? In fact, there is no simple explanation, but a number of different reasons. It didn't happen overnight but over time, beginning with the early enthusiasm for psychoanalysis as a treatment resulting in it being recommended to patients who were not suitable, with disappointing results. This kind of initial, unwarranted optimism is a common occurrence in many disciplines when there is a breakthrough, whether it is in the social or the natural sciences. For example, radical psychosurgery was done in the early days of psychiatry, often with disastrous consequences. Still, with no good alternatives and tragic human suffering, these surgeries were performed. Furthermore, it takes time and experience to discover the limitations of what initially appear to be promising treatments, in part due to the prevalence of temporary placebo effects, and in part due to the complexities of longitudinal outcome studies. In the case of psychoanalysis, this initial optimism was magnified because the procedure was not treacherously invasive, and there were no good alternatives for people who were suffering. It was better to try psychoanalysis than continue treatments known to be ineffective.

In addition to the fact that psychoanalysis was over-prescribed, an unscientific reverence for Freud and his writings contributed to a reluctance to modify how analysis was being conceptualized and conducted. For decades, a religious-like deference to the writings of Freud and his direct disciples had a strangle hold on innovation. Psychoanalytic training continued to emphasize older techniques that failed to keep pace with new developments in the theory, a problem epitomized by the caricature of the analyst who rarely speaks at all. Efforts to innovate were encumbered by an unspoken requirement that new contributions could not challenge Freud's basic ideas, but had to be built upon them. Most publications in psychoanalytic journals, for example, included preliminary references that traced the author's contribution back to Freud. The result: a psychoanalytic science of mind and theories of psychopathology that were very slow to integrate discoveries in related fields like child development, and an inflexible, intensive treatment that lacked efficacy for too many patients.

Around the middle of the twentieth century, the advent of psychiatric medications ushered in a new paradigm for medicine, further marginalizing psychoanalysis. Neurobiological views of psychopathology quickly came to be seen as more scientific. From the beginning, drugs promised a much more effective, efficient, inexpensive, and available treatment for human suffering, to say nothing of the fact that bad brain chemistry is easier for patients to swallow than the challenging work of facing one's conflicts. It's easier to just take a pill. Unfortunately, this initial enthusiasm for medications has also proven overly optimistic, just as with psychoanalysis, and while medications certainly have a place in treating mental illness, ongoing research is making it increasingly apparent that they do not live up to the initial hopes of near magical healing powers. For the most part, these medications do not cure diseases, but treat symptoms related to syndromes of psychopathology.

Last, but not least, the actuarial economics of health insurance and the introduction of managed care (viz. managed "cost") have slowly but surely made psychoanalytic treatment procedures either unworkably micromanaged or not reimbursed at all. This change in the health insurance landscape has favored short-term, symptom-oriented treatments like cognitive-behavioral therapy; "manualized" procedures that can be simplified in step-by-step manuals, requiring much less training, far fewer sessions, and performed by providers at a lower pay scale. If this were not enough, these new short-term treatments were offered not merely as inexpensive substitutes but as superior to the intensive, individualized, self-exploration of psychoanalysis and the psychoanalytic psychotherapies. The result: psychoanalysis became an increasingly marginalized, misunderstood, insular profession dominated by complex conceptual theories and a lack of empirical support. I would wager that most psychoanalysts, when asked what they do, have become familiar with responses like, "People still do that?" or "You still use a couch?"

So why bother trying to revitalize Freud's contributions? What does he offer that merits such efforts? If his ideas are still important, how do we integrate them into all the contemporary mental health fields? Well, this book is intended to be one response to all these questions; a step toward making sure we do not lose the potential for Freud's contributions to inform all contemporary efforts to promote mental health. My plan is to show how his discoveries of psychotherapeutic actions are relevant to *all* contemporary forms of talking therapy, and not only relevant but instructive. Freud gave us the means to isolate and identify the various therapeutic components that contribute to psychotherapeutic change, no matter what the approach to treatment. At the same time, Freud's appreciation of the importance of the therapist-patient relationship in the therapeutic process, one of the reasons for the frequent sessions and the longer duration of most psychoanalytic treatments, helps us understand some of the unavoidable limitations of short-term psychotherapies without being critical of them. Such understanding facilitates the establishment of realistic goals for short-term psychotherapies, goals that do not depend on therapeutic actions that require the immersion in an intensive therapeutic relationship.

Demonstrating Freud's contributions to understanding all psychotherapeutic treatments requires a fresh approach to his work. For the most part, psychoanalysis has tended to develop progressively rather than cumulatively, with new ideas replacing older ones, and old ideas persisting without integration. As Kuhn (2012) pointed out, science tends to progress with those invested in familiar ideas shunning new ones. Consequently, we do not have a composite theory of therapeutic actions that incorporates all of Freud's discoveries. In fact, he himself did not update and incorporate his previous thinking with each new idea. For example, his writings on the technique of psychoanalytic treatment were completed before some of his most important discoveries about the mind, and he never updated them according to his later ideas. One consequence was the perpetuation of the silent analyst, trained to stay out of the way, based on an earlier theory that the patient's unconscious mind would only reveal itself when frustrated. It was not until forty-three years after Freud's death that the problem of the technique of analytic treatment failing to keep pace with Freud's later concepts of the mind and psychopathology was addressed directly (Gray, 1982). Unfortunately, Freud's tendency to move onto new ideas, leaving the old ones aside or behind, has continued. As a result, Freud's discovery of multiple therapeutic actions is concealed by a proliferation of subsequent theories that to various degrees are not new, or are not integrated into his discoveries.

I will show how, by paying careful attention to the evolution of Freud's thinking, it is possible to derive basic modalities of psychotherapeutic action that are generic and revealing of the means by which all "talking cures" have a therapeutic impact. They are ingredients for deconstructing and comparing all psychotherapies, as well as differentiating different approaches to psychoanalysis. They provide a basis for determining and recommending approaches to treatment that are more likely to be effective with a given patient. They even can guide an approach to the treatment of couples. Lastly, these basic modes of therapeutic action have implications for training mental health professionals and for psychotherapy research. Given that these generic modes of therapeutic action are derived from Freud's ideas, psychoanalysis is more relevant today than it has ever been.

To accomplish this appreciation for Freud's lost legacy of therapeutic action, it is necessary to set aside the idea that his newer ideas should replace older ones, or that his newer ideas are superior to older ones, and instead take his body of work as a whole. With this approach, it is possible to discern six distinctive generic modalities of therapeutic action, each one equally important in its own right. These six basic modes of therapeutic action are elementary to all forms of psychotherapy and psychoanalysis, making it possible to identify and compare the essential ingredients of all talking cures, including psychotherapies that are supportive, behavioral, cognitive-behavioral, cathartic, etc. From the shadows, a facet of Freud's genius emerges, and his body of work can take its rightful place at the center of all forms of psychotherapy, with psychoanalytic treatments being only one outcome of psychoanalytic science.

While I believe this legacy is potentially there to be found, what are the challenges and means to uncover it? Freud aspired to develop psychoanalysis into a general science of the human mind as well as a treatment for mental illness. Even if contemporary psychoanalysts agree that in its heyday, Freud's vision for psychoanalysis was overly ambitious, few today would argue that psychoanalysis is sufficiently known, understood, and utilized. In the eyes of the general public, not to mention many professionals and academics trying to understand and treat mental illness, psychoanalysis is often unfamiliar, or worse, it is misperceived and maligned as antiquated and unscientific. To counteract these misperceptions, to reengage the public and the mental health community, it is important we develop the diversity of psychoanalytic discoveries into a more cogent body of psychoanalytic knowledge, and then find ways to demonstrate its current applications. It is important that these applications extend beyond psychoanalytic circles.

What follows is one such effort; beginning with a classification of Freud's fundamental contributions to therapeutic action, followed by a demonstration of how this basic psychoanalytic knowledge is relevant to understanding all forms of psychotherapy, and then a demonstration of the link between diagnosis and treatment recommendations as well as a clinical illustration of these therapeutic actions during psychotherapy.

Finally, these six modes of therapeutic action are used to differentiate various psychoanalysts' views of the *analytic treatment process*, a process that refers to the ways in which the analyst engages with the patient to bring about the desired outcome of the psychoanalytic treatment.

Needless to say, any effort to relate different approaches to psychotherapy and various views of the psychoanalytic process is easier said than done, in part because there are so many different theories and treatment methods, made even more alien because of idiosyncratic terminologies; as a result, it is often difficult to know where the similarities and differences truly lie. The need for a common language of basic modalities of therapeutic action was highlighted by a panel debate, at the meetings of the American Psychoanalytic Association, on different views of therapeutic action within psychoanalysis (Ellman, 2000). According to the panel report, there were numerous differences between the participants on the panel. Concerns were raised as to whether or not a particular model is developmental; is it non-unconscious, non-preconscious, non-conscious, and in fact non-mental; is it neurobiological but not psychoanalytic; or is it more applicable to work with specific kinds of patients? Some panelists felt that we may never have a comprehensive model of therapeutic action, which might be a good thing, whereas others felt there is enough agreement to arrive at a consensual view. They did not consider, however, that it is inherently faulty to speak of "therapeutic action" as a unified concept, and that it is such reductionism that fosters a dysfunctional scientific culture, one where different views compete with each other for correctness. If, instead, we conceptualize talking cures in terms of multiple "therapeutic actions," we avoid this conceptual muddle.

There are two considerations, however, that are critical to understand and compare different systems of psychotherapeutic treatment. First, there is the challenge that different systems employ different terminologies, different languages that can obscure their similarities and differences. This problem is most apparent in language itself: "Oui" in French and "Ja" in German both mean yes, but without knowing both, communications and understanding become impossible. Just as the French and German can have difficulty communicating with each other, so can the psychoanalysts and the behaviorist. Even psychoanalysts of different schools of thought have such difficulties. So we need a universal language of therapeutic actions.

Even more important, however, is the reality that all talking cures have their effects by virtue of more than one therapeutic factor, and while the same basic therapeutic factors are common to all treatments, they are applied in different proportions. Thus, one way to move toward greater understanding is by classifying various "talking cures" according to their basic modes of therapeutic action, relying on Freud's legacy to provide a common ground and a common language. In this way, it can be possible to compare psychoanalytic and non-psychoanalytic approaches to treatment. Ask yourself, when two people get together and participate in talking, with the aim of curing, can it really be the case that the processes are all so essentially different? Might it be the case that similarities between psychotherapeutic treatments are obscured by theorists' desires to be known for their own discoveries, to invent their own terms? How much is truly new and innovative? Frank and Frank (1991) emphasized this in their book, *Persuasion and Healing*, in which they delineate what they feel is common to all talking cures.

During his lifetime, I find that Freud pioneered six basic modes of psychotherapeutic action, and even though at different times he emphasized one mode of therapeutic action over others, and even though he did not equally identify each one independently as a mode of therapeutic action, each one still identifies a means to real psychotherapeutic gain. Unfortunately, the importance of all six modes of therapeutic action has not been emphasized, in part due to Freud's wish to find one that could be the central modality of treatment. While he gave lip service to the value of his previous theories of therapeutic action, he clearly moved on in the hopes of finding one that would be the essence of psychoanalysis as a treatment. At the same time, Freud found that in conducting psychoanalysis, where the goal of treatment is to make the unconscious conscious, some modes of therapeutic action are contra-indicated.

In fact, there can be a conflicting relationship between different modes of therapeutic action, wherein the more treatment emphasizes one mode, the less others are possible or desirable. If, for example, you want to track where someone's thoughts go without any influence of the therapist, in order to see how their mind works, you do not want to give them advice. Freud appreciated this particular hazard and cautioned against using his earlier therapeutic techniques when he developed psychoanalysis as a treatment. When he abandoned suggestion and hypnosis, he warned that such techniques would interfere with the new methods of free association and dream analysis. As a result, the therapeutic usefulness of all his discoveries was subordinated to his focus on advancing psychoanalysis, and the significance of his earlier discoveries got marginalized. But, if we take all his ideas as a multifactorial composite, we find six basic modes of psychotherapeutic action, and another facet of Freud's genius emerges; one that is sorely needed if we are to make sense of the proliferation of so many different theories and approaches to talking cures.

What we find is that cognitive-behavioral therapy, behavioral psychotherapies, supportive psychotherapies, and various psychoanalytic treatments, in fact all psychotherapies, rely on the same modes of therapeutic action that Freud pioneered a century ago. Consequently, these six basic modes of therapeutic action offer a way to begin to classify the compound therapeutic mechanisms of various systematic approaches to treatment. Where psychoanalysis is concerned, it is an approach that offers much more specificity than dichotomous views limited to asking if treatment works more by achieving *insight* or by curative factors in the *therapeutic relationship*. This is by no means to dismiss the substantial body of literature about the therapeutic action(s) of psychoanalytic treatments (see chapter 6). Jones (1997), for example, wrote an article titled "Modes of Therapeutic Action," but rather than seeking to identify separate components that contribute to the effect(s) of *all* treatments, he focused on creating a model that integrates various psychoanalytic techniques. There was annother important contribution on modes of therapeutic action by Frank and Frank (1991) as well as Gabbard and Westen (2003); in the spirit of extending psychoanalytic knowledge, they reach beyond psychoanalysis to include psychoanalytic psychotherapies.

My intent is to reach in a different direction: first, in chapter 2 by extracting six generic modes of psychotherapeutic action from Freud's body of work and extending this basic psychoanalytic knowledge to *all* forms of psychotherapy, including the treatment of couples; second, in chapter 3 by demonstrating the value of linking these basic modes of therapeutic action to the kind of structural and dynamic psycho-diagnoses derived from psychological testing; third, in chapter 4 by using these modes of action to show how they can reveal the curative factors within the complex, detailed processes of a psychoanalytic treatment; fourth, in chapter 5 by showing how these basic modes of therapeutic action can inform the conceptualization and treatment of psychotherapy with couples; and last, by deconstructing different psychoanalysts' views of the *analytic process* according to their emphasis and deemphasis on the six modes of therapeutic action. What emerges is a psychoanalytic approach, based on Freud's original thinking, that respects the value of all modes of therapeutic action and all talking cures.

What we reclaim is the lost legacy of Freud's seminal contributions to how talking cures. With this basic knowledge and common language of psychotherapeutic action, we can stop engaging in bogus controversies over which talking cures are better, and instead engage as one interdisciplinary community, working together to understand the human psyche and all the treatments that alleviate human suffering. Do keep in mind, as you read the next chapter, that while it is based on Freud's life's work, he did not conceptualize these six generic modes of therapeutic action as I have done. While in some cases, a particular mode of therapeutic action, like insight, is more explicitly related to his theories, in others the modes of therapeutic action I define are embedded in his thinking, but they are not so clearly defined in his writings as such.

TWO

Six Generic Modes of Therapeutic Action

A careful examination of the written history of Freud's scientific discoveries reveals an approach initially centered on creating theories of and treatments for psychopathology. Later on he expanded his writing to include general theories of the mind. At every stage in his thinking, each theory is accompanied by a different basis for understanding psychopathology, and, in some cases, a new view of treatment and therapeutic action. Freud freely modified or changed his thinking when a given theory of mental illness lacked explanatory power, or when an approach to treatment lacked therapeutic efficacy. He had a dogged curiosity for figuring out why his patients were not improving or why the benefit of a given treatment was not lasting. Unlike his followers, who held his ideas with a religious-like reverence, Freud was quite willing to replace old theories with new ones.

But what does it mean to call his ideas "theories"? Let us make sure that there is no confusion about what is meant by a theory. In many dictionaries, theory is defined as *a coherent group of tested general propositions, commonly regarded as correct, that can be used as principles of explanation and prediction for a class of phenomena.* In other words, theory does not mean untested, vague, unscientific, or highly speculative, though any or all of these qualifiers could be the case. Theories organize and make meaning of observations. Where the mind is concerned, theories are the most definitive we can get. Thus, it is more correct to speak of validated versus invalidated theories, than to speak of theories versus facts. The point here is to appreciate that referring to Freud's discoveries as theories does not diminish their importance or their scientific validity. Over the course of his lifetime, Freud's theorizing went through many stages with radical developments in his thinking. Taken as a whole, the body of his work tells us a great deal about how talking cures.

Let me very briefly, and at the expense of much important detail, outline the succession of his theorizing about mental illness and treatment. At the beginning of his clinical practice, when he was newly graduated from medical school, Freud relied on existing treatment methods like the "rest cure," which was sometimes combined with electrical stimulation. These treatments were recommended for conditions like neurasthenia or what today would be referred to as depression (for Freud theoretically a *physical fatigue* of nervous origin). The goal of treatment was to build physical stamina and discourage the secondary gains of the illness. In treating these depressed and anxious patients, Freud was struck by the irrational and negative nature of their thinking. He asked himself what would cause people to view their reality as so much worse than it really was. These observations led Freud to theorize that these patients suffered from what he called *antithetical thoughts*. The treatment he devised involved the doctor combatting the antithetical, negative thoughts with conscious suggestion at first, and then later he added hypnotic suggestion. When the outcome of these treatments continued to be disappointing, he next theorized that the pathogenic agent was *strangulated affect*, rooted in real psychological traumas in the past. He theorized that hysterics suffered from reminiscences. The treatment was to release the blocked emotions by catharsis through hypnosis, the reliving of the trauma. Again, he was dissatisfied with the efficacy of the treatment and he doubted that real trauma could be so frequent.

At this point, his theorizing led to the beginning of psychoanalysis. The patient's suffering was now viewed as caused by *unconscious wishes* that were pathogenically repressed due to their primal nature, as opposed to being caused by real emotional traumas. The treatment involved bringing unacceptable unconscious wishes into consciousness by the psychoanalytic method. Still, some patients failed to improve, and in some cases even get worse, leading Freud to theorize the existence of *unconscious conflicts* that could be made conscious and worked through by the psychoanalytic method. Thus, not just the wish but also the patient's objections to the wish could both be unconscious. Thus, it was possible for a patient to suffer with desires and guilt, both being unconscious, resulting in symptomatic suffering, a kind of disguised penance. Again, the treatment involved making the unconscious conscious through the methods of psychoanalysis.

Unfortunately, as Freud went from one theory to another, he did not systematically update his recommendations for clinical technique with every new theory of mind and psychopathology. While his overall approach was to link the theory of mind to treatment and therapeutic action, he did not devote careful thought to the comparison, much less the integration, of the various approaches to therapeutic action that he discovered along the way. Rather than emphasize a cumulative vision of his discoveries of therapeutic action, rather than view treatment as comprised of multiple modes of therapeutic action, Freud's approach emphasized linking a treatment method and clinical theory to a theory of the mind. As a result, psychoanalysts have tended to view his development of new modes of therapeutic action as replacing earlier, inferior ones. Even though the idea of integrating Freud's contributions at different stages of clinical theory has been recognized within psychoanalysis (Gedo and Goldberg, 1973; Sandler, 1974), it has not been extended to integrating Freud's basic knowledge of psychotherapeutic actions into all talking cures; it is this all-encompassing application of Freud's theories that represents a lost legacy, a ground-breaking contribution of psychoanalysis to the mental health fields, more relevant today than it was when Freud was alive.

CONTEXTUALIZING FREUD'S CONTRIBUTIONS

Based on a careful review of the course of Freud's career, there are six basic modes of therapeutic action to be found in his theories. Understand, however, he did not identify them as such. He chose to approach psychology as a discoverer who travels in search of the next find, rather than as a historian who looks back and seeks meaning. He did not work with the benefit of being able to compare many different types of talking cures. He searched without a map. My interpretations of Freud's contributions to therapeutic action are only possible in light of subsequent discoveries in psychology, psychoanalysis, and more recently the neurosciences. Still, these ideas are basically Freud's. Each of the six modes of therapeutic action that I define will be explicitly linked to his evolving methods of clinical technique, highlighting how he emphasized different modalities of therapeutic action at different stages of his theorizing. He just never took them all as representing ingredients that can be used in different proportions to create distinctive approaches to talking cures; each approach based on the best fit between the therapeutic actions and the patient's psychopathology.

While clinical technique refers to the method of the treatment, the action itself refers to the mechanism(s) by which the treatment accomplishes its goals. In fact, these six basic modes of therapeutic action are the ingredients of established schools of treatment, and since there is nothing new here—these basic modes of therapeutic action are fundamental to existing approaches to psychoanalysis and psychotherapy—there is no need for new terminologies. In fact, Freud had a grasp on different modes of action at each stage of his thinking, but because he did not take an integrative approach, he left a legacy where being eclectic can be mistakenly confused for a lack of conviction or an adherence to outdated ideas. In fact, Freud was not *wrong* at any period of his thinking. At each stage he was describing modes of therapeutic action that can be beneficial, given the right fit between patient, treatment, and the treatment goals.

Before getting into the specifics of the six therapeutic actions, however, three more important considerations need to be mentioned. First, these six modes of therapeutic action are basic, meaning they are conceptually fundamental, not that they are simple or irreducible. The metaphor of a recipe and the ingredients used in cooking is useful here, where there are basic ingredients (e.g., eggs, flour, etc.), but the ingredients are themselves complex. The same is true for the basic modes of therapeutic action. Basic does not mean uncomplicated, nor that these modes work in simple, straightforward ways, nor that it is easy to train someone in how to employ them.

Second, while these basic modes of action are building blocks of the therapeutic mechanisms of all systematic approaches to psychoanalysis and psychotherapy, such complex interventions cannot be reduced to these basic modes of therapeutic action. It is safer to assume that there are multifaceted interactions among the various basic modes of action, including the likelihood that increasing some modes may undermine the therapeutic potential of others. Thus, it is important to assume that there is a gestalt created by the blend of therapeutic actions that cannot be understood merely by adding them up. To complicate matters even more, it is also likely that this gestalt is shaped in part by the individual make-up of each patient-therapist pair. Again, basic does not mean simple.

Third, these six basic modes of therapeutic action are Freud's legacy, and do not account for later psychoanalytic developments from self-psychology, object-relations theory, the intersubjective theories, to name but a few; so it may be the case that more basic modes of action need to be added to the list. Beyond psychoanalysis, there are contributions from other systems of thought in psychology like behaviorism, and other fields like the neurosciences. All these subsequent contributions notwithstanding, the significance and scope of Freud's contributions are remarkable, especially when the basic therapeutic actions embedded in his work are extracted and defined separately.

What follows are my definitions of six basic modes of therapeutic action. While I include the direct references to Freud that I relied on to delineate each definition, there are no direct citations for these specific definitions. Rather they are my attempt to summarize the essence of the six modes of therapeutic action (of course, they will unavoidably overlap with numerous definitions used by others in the literature). Following each definition, I will directly relate the mode of therapeutic action to contemporary approaches to psychotherapy that emphasize one particular action over others. While all these therapeutic actions are derived from Freud's work, many of the treatments cited are not psychoanalytic, demonstrating the generic nature of these basic therapeutic actions.

Direct Support

The therapist's direct action and/or intervention in the patient's emotional, cognitive, and/or external life, in order to support adaptive functions that the patient cannot autonomously initiate, manage, or sustain. Such direct support may take the form of providing a therapeutic relationship that facilitates the internal, psychological development of a patient by facilitating other, mutative forms of therapeutic action.

Years before Freud invented psychoanalysis, there were forms of direct support that psychiatrists were employing to care for patients with psychiatric problems. These were the accepted treatments of his day, and much safer than radical, experimental procedures like psychosurgery. One example he cites was the Weir Mitchell therapeutic procedure (Freud, 1887). Known as the rest cure, or bed rest cure, it was a nineteenth-century treatment for many mental disorders, particularly hysteria and depression. "Taking to bed" and becoming an "invalid" for an indefinite period of time was a culturally accepted response to some of the adversities of life. In addition to bed rest, patients were secluded from all family contact in order to reduce dependence on others. The only human that bed rest patients were allowed to see was the nurse who massaged, bathed, and clothed them. Some patients were also not allowed to use their hands at all. In extreme cases electrotherapy was prescribed. The food the patient was served usually consisted of fatty dairy products in order to revitalize the body with new energy. This cure was mainly recommended to women, who more commonly presented with these symptoms. While Freud did not specify how these forms of direct support and intervention in the patient's life could facilitate internal change, as they were not treatments he devised, early in his career he believed that the recovery could be lasting.

Freud did integrate some forms of direct support into his own discoveries. The couch, for example, was seen as a way to facilitate patients' ability to express what went through their minds in as open and uncontrolled a way as possible. The couch removed the social pressures of face-to-face interactions, and by creating a relaxed position minimized the physical in favor of the mental. The recommendation that the doctor not engage in a typically mutual relationship, and instead abstain from personal involvement, might also be considered a kind of support that facilitates the examination of the patient's inner world, without the intrusion of the doctor's personal life. Freud on occasion even went so far as to give a patient food and to take a patient on vacation with him, though these practices did not become a typical aspect of psychoanalytic treatments.

Nowadays, there are many ways in which psychotherapeutic treatments incorporate elements of direct support. While the relative emphasis or deemphasis of direct support varies greatly depending on the treatment approach, it can be found in many actions, including but not limited to hospitalization, medications, giving advice, fee reductions, creating a facilitating atmosphere in our consulting rooms, accommodating a patient's availability for appointment times, and scheduling additional appointments when needed. The rigorous maintenance of confidentiality is an essential form of direct support. Psychoanalysts frequently have separate exits and entrances so patients have privacy, and while no longer essential for a treatment to be considered psychoanalysis, there is still the use of the couch.

The compassionate rationality of the therapist/analyst is also an inevitable form of direct support. Bryan Bird (1972, p. 285) described such direct assistance during psychoanalysis as follows: "One of the most serious problems of analysis is the very substantial help which the patient receives directly from the analyst and the analytic situation. For many a patient, the analyst in the analytic situation is in fact the most stable, wise, and understanding person he has ever met, and the setting in which they meet may actually be the most honest, open, direct, and regular relationship he has ever experienced." While Bird viewed direct help as problematic for psychoanalytic treatment, as was typical when the contemporaneous debate favored *insight* over therapeutic actions related to a *therapeutic relationship*, he did recognize the inevitable existence of such direct support, even in psychoanalysis.

In some cases, however, the most appropriate treatment emphasizes direct support. Sometimes what a patient most needs is some good advice, a different way to look at a problem, or even some specific recommendations about what to do. These may be quite short-term interventions, especially in cases where problems are situational and temporary. Sometimes what patients need is encouragement to trust their own conclusions, so they will have confidence in and follow their own council. On the other hand, sometimes patients will need ongoing direct support, like when chronic, debilitating mental illnesses like schizophrenia compromise an appreciation of reality, resulting in lifelong challenges to good judgment, planning, and anticipation. The same can be true of patients who struggle with very limited intellectual resources. In such cases, the therapeutic actions of direct support may provide situational assistance, without any lasting change in the patient's capacities. Of course, it may be the case that some advice can be generalized to new situations, but in some cases it just is not possible for the therapy to provide independence from a reliance on the therapist. Where this is unavoidably caused by the patient's limitations, it is crucial that the treatment not be disparaged for failing to provide lasting changes.

Last but not least, there are more contemporary theories that profess that direct support can facilitate internal development through the provision of a "holding environment" (Modell, 1976; Winnicott, 1960), "containing" (Bion, 1970), a "self-object relationship" (Kohut, 1972), or a "therapeutic relationship" (Jacobson, 1993), to name a few. These theories of the therapeutic aspects of treatment relationship vary, but in each case the direct provision of some relational need(s) is intended to be more than supportive, often by facilitating the patient's ability to utilize other, mutative forms of therapeutic action like identification and insight. These theories assert that it may not be too late to provide adult patients with emotional, developmental needs that were lacking during their childhoods. Instead of thinking the formative years are over, that critical periods have passed, these theories recommend a kind of delayed parenting that can have the potential of facilitating emotional maturation. Thus, in a way that has long been accepted for the treatment of children and adolescents, these theories claim the therapist/analyst can be a developmental object to the adult patient. While these theories of the analyst/therapist being a developmental object post-date Freud, and he was for the most part opposed to such theories in his time, they do coincide with his view that the therapeutic actions of direct support can be lasting.

Introjection

> *The patient's internalization of the authority of some aspect(s) of the therapist and/or the therapy, which can be permissive, pleasurable, restrictive, and/or unpleasurable, creating a new voice or enhancing an existing voice in the patient's mind. Introjects make it possible to carry on internal relationships based on experiences/perceptions of actual relationships.*

Early on in his career, Freud (1892) observed the apparent irrationality of the thinking that accompanied his patients' suffering. He created a clinical theory about these irrational ideas and symptoms based on the premise that these patients suffered from "subjective uncertainty" and what he labeled "distressing antithetical ideas." While he did not explain the origins of this distorted thinking, he did view it as the source of the patient's suffering. The challenge became how to rectify this pathological thinking and restore rationality. He had to develop a treatment method, which meant he had to find an action that would be therapeutic.

At first he tried direct suggestions to counter these antithetical ideas. The doctor would literally tell the patient which thoughts were irrational, offer rational ones, and encourage the patient to adopt the reasonable ones. When this failed to achieve the success Freud was seeking, he later added hypnotic suggestion in an effort to make a stronger impression. His clinical method was to identify the antithetical ideas, the irrational thoughts, and then to offer conscious suggestions as well as subliminal, hypnotic ones. The therapeutic action was the establishment of a new attitude in the patient's mind, based on the authority of the doctor; an attitude that would be rational and mitigate the patient's belief in irrational, distressing ideas. The patient was encouraged to practice this rational thinking to reinforce it. In the parlance of psychoanalytic theory, such internalized attitudes, established through relationships, bearing the authority of the other person, are referred to as introjects; thus, the mode of therapeutic action is introjection.

Cognitive-behavioral therapy is the prime example of a contemporary treatment that relies heavily on introjection for therapeutic action. The negative thoughts of the cognitive-behavioral model parallel the antithetical ideas of Freud's thinking during this period. The therapist's voice and the methods of countering the irrational beliefs, reinforcing the patient's inner struggle against these beliefs, are the mainstay of therapeutic action. While his approach did not have the benefit of all the subsequent discoveries in behaviorism, and it did not have all the research documentation of contemporary cognitive-behavioral treatments, it does seem in essence quite similar. In fact, it seems no exaggeration to say that in 1892, Freud was the first cognitive-behavioral therapist.

While introjection is deemphasized in psychoanalytic treatments, in favor of other modes of therapeutic action, patients can internalize the authority as well as the imagined authority of their analytic therapists. In the way that children take in both their real experiences with their parents, as well as their fantasied versions of their parents, analytic patients do the same. In fact, in analytic treatments the therapist remaining relatively anonymous encourages the patient's imagination. These fantasies are hopefully a potential source of increased self-awareness, but if they remain unanalyzed they can be introjected. It is not uncommon to hear patients in analytic treatments describe situations where they "heard" their analysts' voice in their mind, and found it helpful in dealing with a situation; still, introjection is typically minimized as a mode of therapeutic action due to psychoanalytic goals of insight and independence.

In the treatment of post-traumatic stress disorder (PTSD), especially for war veterans, a treatment derived from cognitive-behavioral therapy, called Cognitive Processing Therapy, emphasizes this discovery of irrational thoughts and the conscious substitution of more rational ones. Again, there is a process involving the authority of the therapist, and the internalization of more rational cognitive processes, not dissimilar from Freud's early ideas about replacing "antithetical thoughts," ones which he felt did not make sense, with more reasonable ones.

By comparison, in supportive treatments introjection can be very desirable by promoting the patient's independence from the treatment sessions. In a sense, once the therapist comes to be reliably established in the patient's mind, the therapist is available when needed. Patients will talk about how they have a kind of inner dialogue with their therapist. While there is certainly no consensus over the stability of such introjects, for some patients, the reliance on them can last a lifetime, perhaps with occasional treatment sessions to strengthen the mental presence of the therapist.

Catharsis

The patient's direct experience and expression of emotion.

Freud (1893), working with his colleague Josef Breuer, created a theory of psychopathology and treatment, referred to as the affect-trauma model. They theorized that certain psychiatric symptoms they observed, largely conversion hysteria in women, were caused by real trauma experiences, blocked from expression by the patient's mind. They felt this blockage prevented the abreaction of the emotions, leading to "strangulated affect" and symptom formation. Under light hypnosis, the strangulated affect was brought into consciousness, promoting abreaction and symptomatic relief. The mechanism of therapeutic action, catharsis, was the expression of emotion or abreaction, the reliving of a traumatic experience in order to purge it of its emotional excesses.

This treatment method, devised by Freud and Breuer over one hundred years ago, as a way to treat the traumatic neuroses, now referred to as post-traumatic stress disorders (PTSDs), has stood the test of time. In cases of PTSD, for example, imaginal or in-vivo behavioral exposure therapies are used to encourage abreaction. The patient is encouraged to think of the situation that is associated with the trauma, or in some cases the behavioral therapist goes with the patient to the situation of the trauma, in order to stir up the emotion in order that it can be mastered. One such treatment that has gained recognition in the treatment of war veterans is called Prolonged Exposure Therapy, in which the patient is repeatedly exposed to the painful affects associated with their trauma, including listening to audiotapes of the treatment sessions in between meetings.

To really understand such exposure treatments that promote catharsis, it is important to understand the current psychoanalytic signal theory of affects. Anxiety, for example, is understood to be a signal of danger. If all goes well, the anxiety leads to an adaptive response that removes the danger, and the anxiety is reduced. If, however, the anxiety becomes so great as to compromise the ability to think, it can no longer serve a signal function and becomes overwhelming. The result is emotional trauma. This can lead to a tendency to avoid anything associated with the trauma, which can further result in depression and other forms of psychopathology, including anxiety, nightmares, phobias, etc. Being able to return to the unprocessed emotion in therapeutic and non-traumatic settings promotes mastery of the trauma and relief from its symptoms.

In addition to traumatic stress disorders, the benefits of emotional expression for unresolved grief reactions has also been demonstrated (Greenberg et al., 1996), as has the facilitation of grief reactions in cases where the grieving process has been arrested, resulting in symptoms like depression, denial of loss, avoidance of moving on in life, etc. When the loss of a loved one is not mourned, when the grief is avoided, a number of problems can ensue. Like the person who is hobbled by the failure to recover from a physical injury, the person who fails to grieve lives a life that will in some way be hobbled. This can take different forms, like the displacement of the loss so that someone alive but not easily available is missed, instead of the person who died, thereby creating a situation where a reunion is not hopeless. The death of a child, or sometimes even the child growing up and leaving home, can result in reactions where a parent insists the child's room must remain unchanged, expressing an unconscious wish that the child will return and all will be as it was. An extreme psychotic version of pathological grief was portrayed in Alfred Hitchcock's movie *Psycho*, where the son performs taxidermy on his mother and takes on her identity alongside his own, acting out their relationship and thereby preserving it as well as her.

Beyond PTSD and pathological grief, catharsis also has a place in supportive, behavioral, cognitive-behavioral, eye movement and desensitization and reprocessing (EMDR), exploratory psychotherapies as well as psychoanalysis. If a failure to deal with emotions is the primary problem, and catharsis is easily achieved, the therapy might be relatively short-term. But where there are extensive resistances to emotional expression, or where emotional expression leads to problematical or dangerous reactions, there may be a need for more frequent sessions and more intensive treatment. The avoidance of distressing emotions can take many forms, but whatever form it takes, avoidance is a powerful source of resistance to treatment. Why? Because there is always relief at the moment of avoidance; there is no longer the need to face the conflict. But even more pathogenic is that there is no longer the opportunity to experience and master that which is being avoided. Imagined dangers, for example, will not be exposed as unreal. In some cases, if the patient continues to avoid, the treatment itself may not be possible.

Insight

> The patient's gaining self-awareness about feelings, thoughts, perceptions, fantasies, and patterns of behavior previously unknown, repressed, unappreciated, or misunderstood, opening up new perspectives and emotional/cognitive/behavioral possibilities, which serves as an important component in the development of a psychologically minded, self-reflective attitude.

Many of Freud's theories include some form of insight as a mode of therapeutic action. One noteworthy example is in "The Ego and the Id," in a footnote where he describes the process of helping patients become aware of and work through the symptomatic expression of an unconscious sense of guilt based on an identification (Freud, 1923). In this expanded definition, insight refers to the therapeutic action of newly acquired self-knowledge, not techniques for acquiring that insight or the autonomous capacity for self-analysis, which refer to methods and goals of treatment rather than the mode of therapeutic action. Surely the capacity for self-analysis includes both insight and identification with the analyst's analyzing function, so it is not reducible to one generic mode of therapeutic action.

For years, beginning with the advent of the topographic model of the mind in Freud's work (1900), insight was the sine qua non of psychoanalytic treatments. Since Freud believed that symptoms were the result of conflicts in the mind, he needed to theorize a mind with separate structures; the mind had to be divided into something that was in conflict with something else. In the topographic model, the mind was divided into three structures: Unconscious, Preconscious, and Conscious. In other words, the mind and psychopathology was understood as comprised of conflicts between different levels of access to conscious awareness. He postulated that symptoms were the result of repressed pathogenic wishes and memories. This resulted in an approach to treatment that emphasized making the unconscious conscious. Because the structures in the mind were levels of awareness, the importance of relationships, both formative ones during childhood as well as the relationship with the analyst/therapist on the patient during the treatment were deemphasized. In the lingo of a kind of conceptual shorthand, this was referred to as a one-person psychology. The structures in the mind did not represent relationships. In this model, if the analyst was technically able to remain in the background and listen, while the patient said whatever came into his or her mind, Freud felt there would be clues to discovering the repressed pathogenic memories and wishes. Transference was a primary source of insight, when the patient's unconscious conflicts would become manifest in the relationship to the analyst. Once the unconscious conflicts had access to conscious awareness, it would be possible to subject them to reality testing, the conscious ability to distinguish fantasy from reality (a capacity clearly lacking, for example, when we dream and are not conscious).

Subsequently, Freud replaced the topographic model, with its one-person psychology, with the two-person psychology of the structural model (1923) of Id, Ego, and Superego. This revised model of the mind formally incorporated relationships into its structures (e.g., both the ego and the superego being based on identifications, especially with early, important childhood relationships). The importance of relationships came to the forefront with this move away from the repressed pathogenic memories of the topographic model, to the conflicts between animalistic aggressive and sexual drives of the Id, the ideals and prohibitions of the Superego, and the Ego as a structure that is charged to manage a compromise between Id, Superego, and external reality. With this theoretical shift to the structural model, and numerous subsequent theoretical advancements since 1923, there has been growing recognition that it is impossible for the therapist to stand off to the side and observe the patient without influencing what is observed. The importance of early relationships increased, the need to monitor counter-transference became integral to treatment, but insight remained the preferred mode of therapeutic action, though it became increasingly recognized that it is neither possible nor desirable to ignore other modes of therapeutic action.

Apart from psychoanalytic treatments, insight is also a significant component of contemporary, cognitive-behavioral treatments (CBTs) that aim to make one's thinking and behavior more rational. Helping patients to recognize their irrational thoughts, behaviors, and habits, then working with them to find rational ones to compete with the unreasonable patterns, clearly can provide some insight into maladaptive ideas and behaviors. As compared to psychoanalytic approaches, however, CBT does not necessarily pursue insight into the origins and the underlying psychodynamic reasons for the psychopathology. It is sufficient to identify that it is pathological and then to make conscious plans and efforts to engage in thinking and functioning in more adaptive ways.

To the extent that supportive psychotherapies endeavor to maximize the patient's adaptive thinking and behavior, insight can be a component of these treatments as well. When, for example, the supportive therapist offers good judgment to patients who cannot find it within themselves, patients can certainly have moments of insight into the ways that their judgment is wanting, and there is the hope that the insight will be retained and promote better judgment in future situations. Hospitalizing a patient may give them sufficient relief from an immediate crisis and unbearable stressors that they can recover from a regression and resume a higher level of functioning. In the process, it is possible the patient will develop enough insight about the circumstances that led to the regression that they can monitor and avoid its reoccurrence; otherwise, repeated hospitalizations are more likely.

Identification

> *The conscious and/or unconscious internalization of aspects and/or attributes of the therapist and/or the therapy, that leads to a modification in the patient's behavior and subjective experience of themselves, or both. The modification increases the patient's resemblance to aspects of the therapy and/or the therapist, which can promote a self-reflective attitude.*

Freud (1938) remained very cautious about the role of identification in bringing about any lasting therapeutic results. While he recognized that psychoanalysis encourages patients to transfer the authority of the super-ego to the analyst, and that the patient can take on the values of the analysts, he emphasized a view that the therapeutic action of analysis should focus on insight, and he remained suspicious that any therapeutic successes taking place under the sway of positive transference and iden-tification would be suggestive and temporary. Nonetheless, he recog-nized that identification was a factor in the treatment process. One relat-ed consideration is the idea that in some cases, introjection may precede identification. In other words, there can be a process, similar to the one during childhood development, where first the voice of the external au-thority is internalized as an object representation in the mind, and only later does it become a part of the self-representation and identification. To this point, we do not only identify with external objects, but also with internal representations in the mind.

Nowadays there is considerable controversy about the accuracy much less the desirability of continuing to be so skeptical of the therapeutic action of non-interpretative (viz., insight oriented) aspects of the transfer-ence relationship. The work of Blatt (1974, 1992), for example, based on research and a reevaluation of the results of the Menninger Research Project, really captures the increasing recognition of the therapeutic ac-tion based on the therapeutic relationship rather than the acquisition of insight. In describing his findings Blatt says, "These results suggest that we must be aware that the therapeutic context presents at least two major dimensions to patients—a therapeutic relationship and the possibility of insight and understanding" (Blatt and Behrends, 1987). He found that while these two dimensions were intertwined in the therapeutic process, some patients seemed to value and be more responsive to the quality of the therapeutic relationship, while other patients seemed to value and be more responsive to the interpretive activity of the therapist and the pro-cess of insight. He concluded that while most patients undoubtedly gain from both of these therapeutic dimensions, different types of patients are more responsive to insight whereas others are more responsive to the therapeutic relationship. In fact, there are increasing numbers of authors and theoretical points of view that emphasize aspects of the therapeutic relationship; the self-psychological, object-relational, and relational ap-proaches stand out. Some authors, Malin (1966) for example, specifically refer to identification as part of mutative projective identifications that take place in the therapeutic process. Unfortunately, this distinction stirred a debate between the effectiveness of therapeutic actions based on the therapeutic relationship versus those based on insight. Hopefully, by expanding the modes of therapeutic action beyond *insight* versus the *ther-apeutic relationship*, by moving beyond such dichotomous thinking to con-sidering that Freud left us a legacy of six modes of therapeutic action, the debate can be quelled in favor of more specificity and inclusion.

Working Through

> *The application of therapeutic gains from direct support, introjection, cathar-*
> *sis, insight, and identification, both during and outside the treatment sessions,*
> *resulting in repeated encounters with experiential, relational, emotional, and*
> *behavioral changes, reinforcing modifications in the mind and leading to more*
> *stable change over time.*

In 1926, Freud wrote about the difficulties of treatment even after the patient is fully invested in the process and the cure:

> For we find that even after the ego has decided to relinquish its resis-
> tances, it still has difficulty in undoing the repressions; and we have
> called the period of strenuous effort which follows after its praise-
> worthy decision, the phase of *working-through*. The dynamic factor that
> makes a working-through of this kind necessary and comprehensible is
> not far to seek. It must be that after the ego-resistance has been re-
> moved the power of the compulsion to repeat—the attraction exerted
> by the unconscious prototypes upon the repressed instinctual pro-
> cess—has still to be overcome. There is nothing to be said against de-
> scribing this factor as the resistance of the unconscious.

Fenichel (1939) described the classical technique of *working through* as follows: "The ego does not completely relinquish its resistant attitude because of a single demonstration (p. 79). Soon the symptom or neurotic character trait reappears and the entire process outlined above must be repeated. The process that requires demonstrating to patients the same thing again and again at different times or in various connections is called, following Freud, working through (pp. 78-79)." In other words, there must be a process of repeating the changes over and over, until the changes are widely established.

While all talking cures require some working through, behavioral approaches to psychotherapy are primarily based on working through, without necessarily requiring insight for change to take place. While Freud referred to the need to overcome a theoretical compulsion to repeat, the need for repetition in working through parallels two primary laws of behaviorism, originally defined by Thorndike's (1913) theories of connectionism: (1) Law of Effect—responses to a situation which are followed by a rewarding state of affairs will be strengthened and become habitual responses to that situation; and (2) Law of Exercise—connections become strengthened with practice and weakened when practice is discontinued. Nearly forty years later, in an attempt to create a clinical theory that combines behaviorism with Freud's drive theory of psychoanalysis, Dollard and Miller (1950) elaborated on these behavioral principles of reinforcement that make neurotic conflicts resistant to change. They recommended that it is as unwise to reduce human behavior to principles of reinforcement, to ignore basic human drives, as it is to ignore the demonstrated truths of the basic laws of behaviorism.

More recently, discoveries in the neurosciences are being applied to psychoanalytic knowledge (Kandel, 1999), where working through can be related to the differences between *procedural* and *declarative* memory. Again, however, as with Freud's earlier discoveries, the more recent concept of procedural memory is similar to Hartmann's concepts of automization (1939). In fact, there are many concepts that were developed as part of ego psychology and the efforts to understand the adaptive functions of the mind that parallel those of the neurosciences.

There are specific examples of working through in the psychotherapy literature. Sorter (1995), for example, wrote about a case where she utilized the concept of procedural memory to understand and treat a patient as follows: "After many repetitions of the intervention, his anxiety lessened and he developed a bit of humor. No longer did he have to do it himself. The automatic procedure of 'checking' which had operated out of his awareness had now become available for reflective consideration." In other words, this process of "many repetitions" or of *working through* was essential to the therapeutic actions of the treatment. Clyman (1991) describes this working through process for both insight and what he refers to as emotional procedures as follows: "Working through occurs not only through repeated insights, but by trying out new procedures in multiple domains. The new procedures must be practiced in order for them to be elicited automatically (for a related discussion, see Horowitz et al., 1984). Working through modifies emotional heuristics through repeated insights as well as through the direct modification of emotional heuristics by repeated practice."

While Brenner (1987), a most noteworthy American psychoanalyst, once argued that the phobic does not need to be told to do what is feared, that "good analytic work" is all that is needed, he also remarked that *why* psychoanalysis takes so much time is a question which remains unanswered. Considering the laws of behaviorism and the mechanisms of automization or procedural memory, analysis may take longer than necessary because working through, an essential mode of therapeutic action, is insufficiently integrated into "good analytic work." I propose that working through, as defined above and done in a systematic manner, is critical to facilitating analytic progress. Patients need to understand that they are subject to behavioral principles of reinforcement, to the mechanisms of procedural memory, and that a process of working through must accompany analytic gains in order to promote change.

For example, patients can gain the insight that a phobia is caused by the displacement of an unreasonable unconscious fantasy, but they still must face the fearful situations in order to alter the conditioned emotional responses. Over time, their repeated avoidance has had an extremely toxic, cumulative impact. Not only is there the immediate relief of the avoiding what is feared, as if it is a real danger, the patient never gets to find out that the feared outcome does not come true. While the analytic insights can provide the courage, making it understood that the dangers are imagined, the anxieties will likely not abate without the process of working through. Some of this may be done in the treatment sessions, but often it must also be done outside the consulting room. In order to appreciate these realities of talking cures, patients must be educated about the reasons and need for working through.

SUMMARY

A careful examination of Freud's writings about therapeutic action over the course of his career reveals six distinct generic modes of therapeutic action: Direct Support, Introjection, Catharsis, Insight, Identification, and Working Through. While he did not delineate his thinking about therapeutic action in the way I have done, being that his destination was a unified theory of the mind and the human condition, a careful examination of the steps in his journey reveals the significance and contemporary relevance of all his ideas about therapeutic action.

In reality, when two people meet and engage in any form of psychotherapy, no one of these modes of therapeutic action can be the sole mechanism of change, operating in isolation of all the others. For that reason, any form of psychotherapy that claims to be based on only one of these basic modes of therapeutic action will be ignoring the unavoidable impact of others. Still, it is clear that different systems of psychotherapy, like cognitive-behavioral therapy and the various forms of psychoanalytic theory and technique, emphasize and deemphasize different basic modes of action. While there are dozens of books and journal articles written that lay claim to the discovery of a new approach to psychotherapy, often promoting its originality by giving the treatment approach a new name, or by creating new terminologies, I find that the underlying therapeutic actions of these supposedly innovative approaches can be found in the six basic therapeutic actions that Freud emphasized at different points in his career.

What remains is to demonstrate practical applications of this knowledge; so in what follows I will first show how it is possible to use psychological diagnoses based on comprehensive psychological testing to determine which basic modes of therapeutic action are more or less likely to be effective. In other words, how careful and in-depth diagnoses can point the way to the optimal approaches to treatment, according to which basic modes of therapeutic action are emphasized. Next, I will go through a detailed, albeit highly disguised and fictionalized illustration of an in-depth exploratory psychotherapy, in order to demonstrate the actual operation of these basic therapeutic actions during treatment itself. In the next chapter, to demonstrate the application of these generic modes of therapeutic action beyond the psychotherapy of individuals, I will de-

scribe an approach to the treatment of couples that is based on psychoanalytic principles and these modes of therapeutic action. Lastly, and before
some final reflections, I will reference numerous psychoanalytic authors'
definitions of the ways psychoanalysis brings about change, and show
how it is possible to deconstruct and compare these different views according to which basic modes of therapeutic action are more or less emphasized by each author.

THREE

Diagnoses and Therapeutic Action

Depending on a patient's diagnosis or diagnoses, some modes of therapeutic action are more likely to be successful than others. Direct support,
for example, is often needed when a patient is overwhelmed by a crisis,
has extremely limited cognitive resources, or has a severe psychiatric
disorder that compromises the ability to distinguish reality from fantasy,
to name a few. Introjection can be quite effective with patients who have
manifest or underlying dependency needs and hunger for guidance, as
they are prone to internalize the authority of the therapist, giving the
therapist access to a positive influence on the patient's life. Attempts at
catharsis are likely to be very daunting with obsessional patients given
such extensive defenses that function to fend off emotions, to say nothing
of the more challenging alexithymic patients whose emotional detachment often puts their feelings beyond reach. Phobic patients need, but
will find it challenging to do the working through that requires facing
their fears; for them, insight can provide a source of courage, increasing
their confidence that the fears are not realistic. Masochistic patients often
require insight into the underlying dynamics of their need to suffer, without which any therapeutic efforts are likely to end up transformed into
yet more forms of suffering.

These are a few general examples, but in order to truly appreciate the
specificity of linking diagnosis to modalities of therapeutic action, it is
necessary to have a more in-depth, dynamic diagnostic understanding of
the individual than a descriptive diagnosis applied to groups according
to consciously observable phenomena like symptoms, as is the case with
the American Psychiatric Association's contemporary Diagnostic Statisti-
cal Manual (DSM). In an effort to convey this more individualized approach, what follows are excerpts from psychological testing evaluations,

describing in detail the relationship between psychological functioning and choice of therapeutic action.

Before referring to any clinical material, however, I want to address the categorical importance of confidentiality. With very few legal exceptions, all communications between patients and licensed mental health providers are private. It is patients who hold the privilege of telling others about their assessments and treatment. For this reason, in all the clinical examples that follow, the clinical material is deeply disguised and excludes any real identifying information. By emphasizing symptoms, personality organization, internal wishes, fantasies, and conflicts, which can be similar for many people, it is possible to exclude the external, identifying details of a patient's life. If this were not enough, to be even more careful to protect confidentiality, I have included the work of colleagues and supervisees, making it impossible to identify the provider as well.

For the reader who is unfamiliar with psychological tests, and for those unfamiliar with the psychoanalytic approach to psychological testing, a brief orientation will be helpful. First, the tests themselves: the Wechsler Adult Intelligence Sale—Revised (WAIS-R) and the Wechsler Intelligence Scale for Children—Revised (WISC-R) refer to David Wechsler's standardized intelligence tests that measure a number of cognitive functions like abstract thinking, judgment, planning, anticipation, and range of knowledge; the Babcock Story Recall Test is a measure of long-term memory, a cognitive test missing from Wechsler's intelligence tests; the Rorschach inkblot test provides measures of deeper levels of personality organization and unconscious conflicts; the Thematic Apperception Test, or TAT, measures the nature and quality of internal object relations. IQ scores are given as a range to respect that the intelligence tests have an inherent error factor, so an exact number is misleading.

This battery of tests, based on psychoanalytic theory, was first developed by Rapaport, Gill, and Schafer (1945) at the Menninger Foundation, but has since undergone numerous developments and advancements in the nearly seventy years since its initial publication. The value of this psychoanalytic approach lies in the fact that it is not primarily based on nomothetic, statistically based diagnoses, but aims to get at an understanding of the unique, conscious, and unconscious psychological make-up of the individual. Thus, it is not a psychological testing system that can produce computerized test reports, like the Minnesota Multiphasic Personality Inventory (MMPI), which generate conclusions like "most people who give these responses are. . . ." Instead, diagnostic conclusions are individualized, linking specific unconscious conflicts and personality structure to problems of adaptation, thereby permitting more customized recommendations for therapeutic interventions.

For the sake of clarity, I will give examples of evaluations where the individual diagnostic understandings are different, followed by the diagnostic conclusions where I will point out the different modes of therapeutic actions recommended in brackets, so that their rationales will be clear (e.g., [Direct Support] or [Insight]). I will emphasize more salient modes of therapeutic action, so it is important to keep in mind all modes can be involved in any treatment to various degrees. Working Through, for example, will be an essential component of most forms of psychotherapy.

Example 1

Diagnostic Understanding: This mid-adolescent boy is struggling valiantly with a severe depression and a great deal of emotional agitation and distress. While his depression is apparent on all the psychological tests, the impact on his cognitive functioning and memory on the intelligence tests and the test of memory are most immediately striking. Overall, he scores in the 28th percentile on the WAIS-R, with a drop in Performance IQ as compared to Verbal IQ of 17 points (Full Scale IQ of 88-94; Verbal IQ of 97-103; Performance IQ of 78-88). On delayed recall of the Babcock story test of memory he cannot even remember half of the story. He frequently misses easy items and gets harder ones, which is a sign of some cognitive regression. For example, he says there are "127" weeks in a year and that the sun rises "in the West," but he knows who was president of the United States during the Civil War and he knows who wrote Hamlet. In short, there are clear indications of cognitive impairment secondary to his emotional distress.

Alongside this clear evidence of cognitive impairment, the other test indications of depression and feelings of failure and agitation are alarming. On the Rorschach test, for example, he sees "a face screaming." On the WAIS-R picture arrangement test he complicates a simple sequence of a man building a house with the perception that "the man built a house with so many problems he had to go back and rebuild it all over again." On the TAT, he tells stories about a boy who is very disappointed in the birthday gifts his father gives him, about a man who is really at home in a cemetery, about a boy who is very worried about his future, and about someone who is so disappointed in life that she attempted suicide but failed. Clearly underneath a thin veneer of denial he is suffering with a great deal of narcissistic damage related to feeling like a failure, and feeling hopeless about the future. When asked what the saying *shallow brooks are noisy* means, he sadly says, "it means that even weak things can have their strong points."

While there are no manifest indications on the tests of psychosis or a thought disorder, there are indications of considerable identity confusion and a great deal of anger that he cannot express in developmentally mature and adaptive ways, resulting in confusion and helplessness. The ease with which his aggressive and depressive fantasies corrupt his perceptions does speak to some borderline ego pathology, which further contributes to his confusion. On the WAIS-R, for example, he sees a boy-father picture arrangement sequence as one where "the boy is angry," yet this idiosyncratic perception of anger results in a story that really does not make much sense. On the Rorschach test, he sees a fight with a whole bunch of animals battling each other, explaining that the symmetry of the inkblot makes him think the animals on one side of the card are angry that the ones on the other side are copying them, and on the TAT, his rage emerges in two frank stories of murder. Thus, even relatively conflict-free situations are likely to be conflictual for him due to all the internal conflict he is struggling to contain.

He harbors so much anger at feeling neglected, misunderstood, and unimportant, and his inner-outer ego boundaries are sufficiently fluid, that it's hard to know how much his perception of not being special is externally based or caused by the projection of his own aggression. Certainly he feels like a "lost child" and he has a great deal of underlying father hunger for someone who can guide him and who will admire him.

Diagnostic Conclusions: This adolescent boy is in serious emotional trouble. He needs immediate treatment for his depression; otherwise, his cognitive impairments, his school difficulties, his conflicts at home, and his own feelings of being confused and lost related to distinct narcissistic damage are likely to escalate into an even more serious depressive crisis with dangers of his becoming actively suicidal. As it is, he has a potential for suicide that should be monitored [*Direct Support*]. Whatever medications might be considered [*Direct Support*], he will also need ongoing, intensive psychotherapy at least twice weekly to help him attain more developmentally advanced ways of managing his anger [*Introjection, Identification, Insight, and Working Through*]. When his depression is significantly improved, it would be a good idea to have him take the WAIS-R another time to see if there is still marked subtest scatter, and if so pursue a more extensive educational assessment and treatment for learning disabilities [*Direct Support*].

Since he more readily connects his conflicts with aggression and self-criticism to his relationship with his father, treatment with a man is likely to make his conflicts more easily reached, while at the same time providing him with a compassionate, paternal developmental object [*Identification and Introjection*] as well as someone who can help him sort out his feelings [*Catharsis and Insight*]. He needs help separating his own ideals and anger from the actual disappointments in his life, so he can come to have more realistic, integrated perceptions of his parents and make peace with their shortcomings [*Insight*]; only in this way will he be able to work through his disappointments in himself.

Example 2

Diagnostic Understanding: Currently in treatment for a refractory depression, this middle-aged man openly and enthusiastically participated in the administration of the psychological tests, such that the results offer a good indication of his psychological make-up. Taken as a whole, the battery of tests gives no signs of psychopathology that would severely compromise his sense of reality. In fact, his reality testing is intact on tests with considerable external structure like the WAIS-R, and on tests with little external structure like the Rorschach projective test, where a respectable 88 percent of his perceptions are very accurate resemblances of the inkblots. Thus, there are no indications of either psychotic or borderline ego structure.

On the other hand, the extent to which his neurotic character structure is organized around ideational/intellectualized defenses against the awareness of any strong and/or disturbing affects is impressive. On the Rorschach test, for example, although there are instances where some of his sixteen responses are elaborated with ideational fantasy (e.g., "two African women cooking; two girls dancing with their hair flying), there are almost no instances where he can recognize, much less integrate, either the shading or color of the inkblots into his responses (which is the equivalent of integrating affects). Even when a response is clearly influenced by the color or shading of the inkblots, he claims it is only based on the shape (i.e., he cannot recognize the other influences on his own perceptions). Strikingly, 100 percent of his Rorschach responses are determined by the shape of the inkblots, which points to a rigid adherence to facts and external realities rather than emotions and inner realities. In other words, this man has a very limited ability to recognize his own emotions, much less to experience them in a way that is integrated in his own life.

By contrast to his limited "emotional intelligence," his cognitive capacities are impressive. On the WAIS-R he scores in the Superior to Very Superior range or the 96th to 98th percentile (Full Scale IQ of 124-130; Verbal IQ of 126-132; Performance IQ of 114-122). The eleven-point drop in Performance as compared to Verbal subtest scores may point to some depression, but the subtest scores affected concern psychomotor speed (Digit Symbol) and the visual ability to notice missing items in pictures (Picture Completion). By comparison, his concentration and attention are excellent and quite commensurate with his overall IQ, not evidencing any impairment. Also, his memory on the Babcock Story Recall Test, while slightly less than his overall intelligence would predict, is not markedly impaired by any means. Thus, it seems more likely that his weaker cognitive functions are related to motivation and a tendency to disregard details, both of which may relate to the avoidance of strong and/or disturbing emotions (viz., what he does not notice or attend to will not stir up feelings).

Even though this is a very smart man, whose character is organized around defenses that reflexively fend off the awareness of emotions (hence the pleasant themes on the Rorschach test), there is evidence of underlying emotional conflict on the TAT, a test that has a strong projective pull for both affect and conflict. Even on this test, however, his defenses were in full force. Thus, he frequently thought of multiple possibilities of stories to tell about each TAT picture, allowing him to dismiss the significance of any one story that occurred to him. When I asked him to pick one story, he "joked" that I was making it hard for him, and then in some cases could not think of any story at all. He also explicitly commented that he did not want to pick one story since then, "you will include it as part of your data." This strong tendency to dismiss the significance of his own stories (like some people do with their own dreams) certainly points to marked denial and avoidance, both of which can be quite ego syntonic.

While he does not see his own stories as very meaningful, his TAT responses nonetheless portray conflicted themes of unhappiness, a broken heart, and of a wickedly selfish person. In general, the more troubling the story the less he was able to relate it to himself, in keeping with the distancing of emotional conflict.

One card, depicting two women in a position often seen as one strangling the other, he was unable to permit a response because it stirred up so much conflict over aggression. Instead of telling a story, he said, "strange . . . do you know what it is? Odd . . . almost creepy . . . are the answers on the back [viz., the back of the TAT cards]. I don't know! Emotionally disturbed on some level. I don't know what that woman is doing to that woman. Too weird." To another card, with a woman crouched on the ground and a somewhat indistinct object on the floor (often seen as a gun), he told a story of a happy woman daydreaming of a good time. Then, when I asked about the object on the floor, he said, "maybe she's thinking of killing her cat . . . you're not writing that down [said to me] . . . is that a gun?" Here is a rare example of the rage that lurks below the surface of his awareness, despite the fact that he is likely to dismiss his own thought as holding any significance, denying it as merely being a joke.

Diagnostic Conclusions: This is a very bright, neurotically organized man whose capacity to consciously experience and integrate his emotions is extremely limited. Interestingly, when asked to describe his mother he commented that she was "emotionally dishonest," by which he meant that she was unable to deal with conflict and feelings directly ("you never know where you are with her"), so it appears that his character has developed around defenses that complement her preference to avoid emotional conflict. Given what the psychological tests reveal, it is not surprising that his psychiatrist has had great difficulty getting to an understanding of this man's emotional, psychological complexities. Avoidance, rationalization, compartmentalization, possibly somatization, minimization, and denial make it quite difficult to get to his feelings and conflicts, beyond a general depressive malaise and frustration with his physical illnesses.

It is highly likely that there are a number of unresolved areas of conflict, including his emotional reaction to the physical illnesses, which have accumulated over the years. He did describe taking many years to get over a girlfriend when he was younger, which exemplifies his great difficulty dealing with loss and anger and pathological grief.

This man needs but will find it very difficult to tolerate an intensive, expressive [Cathartic], insight-oriented psychotherapy [Insight] that can help him access his emotions and deal with past, present, and future conflicts, including the multiple disappointments in his life. More frequent than once weekly meetings may help bring more affect to the surface, as will confrontations about the details of situations he may prefer to dismiss with generalities. His knowledge that he has had great difficulty dealing with loss and disappointment in the past, as well as his awareness of his surviving parent's difficulty dealing with conflict, may help engage his appreciation for his emotional difficulties. It will be important that he understand his current "malaise" is a diffuse version of more defined conflicts that his mind keeps obscured, along with feelings of anxiety, anger, sadness, and depression. If he cannot tolerate or engage in an exploratory-cathartic treatment, one that has a more cognitive-behavioral emphasis [Introjection and Insight] could help him by increasing his capacity to see the ways his perceptions are negatively distorted by his depression.

Example 3

When I first met this young woman in the waiting room, referred because she had no direction in her life and was involved in self-defeating behaviors, her seeming both shy and assertive at the same time, as if she was trying to mask an underlying fragility with some bravado, touched me. Throughout the testing she was cooperative, again seeming to try to mask narcissistic insecurities when she thought her test responses were inadequate, incomplete, or incorrect; this defensiveness frequently took the form of responding impulsively, leaving little time for reflection or emotion. She was reassured by supportive comments and understanding.

We discussed the fact that she had undergone psychological testing on more than one occasion before, though she could not recall specifically when or the results, and she openly admitted that she had never taken these evaluations seriously and had "BS'd" (sic) the psychologists. I asked if she thought she had any problems and she said, "I have problems with my mood changing so much . . . and I need to learn more about myself." She also said that she planned to take the evaluation with me seriously, and indeed my impression is that she did so. When I asked if she had any plans for the future, she said she had some ideas about working with animals. I administered a battery of psychological tests including WAIS-R, the Babcock Story Recall Test, the Rorschach test, and the TAT. The WAIS-R was chosen over a more recent version of that test because of its greater capacity to be used as a projective instrument.

The results of the WAIS-R clearly reveal one significant if not primary source of this young woman's difficulties. Overall, she scores in the Borderline range of intellectual functioning or at the bottom fifth percentile (Verbal IQ of 67-73; Performance IQ of 81-89; Full Scale IQ of 72-78). Her Verbal subtests are fifteen points lower than her Performance subtests, which is sufficient to indicate a statistically significant difference. Even taking into account that her scores are somewhat lower due to her impulsive approach, largely motivated by the avoidance of emotional exposure to failure, she still has very limited cognitive potential. Her thinking is concrete and tends to be egocentric (e.g., she defines tranquil to mean "a medicine").

Growing up in an upper-middle-class environment must have exposed her to numerous challenges where she was unable to keep up with other children, resulting in years of narcissistic injury, likely a source of cumulative narcissistic trauma. Moreover, she is severely limited in her capacity to put her inner experience and her world into words, making it difficult for her to think about her feelings, much less to plan and reflect on her reactions. It's also likely that her adoptive parents possess far greater intellectual resources, which may have disrupted the basic attachment between them from her early years. The higher Performance IQ is consistent with her being predisposed to action more than thinking, while her low scores on Picture Arrangement, combined with the low score on Comprehension, point to her difficulties having her actions guided by reasonable judgment and anticipation. One caveat: it is not clear to what extent daily marijuana and alcohol abuse may be reducing her intellectual functioning, though she is still very limited.

Her long-term memory, 48 percent immediate recall and 38 percent delayed recall as measured by the Babcock Story Recall Test, is consistent with Borderline intelligence, and further support that the WAIS-R measure of her limited cognitive functioning is accurate. She is not going to easily retain information, especially if it is at all abstract. Furthermore, the fact that she twice recalled "a man cut his hand" to be "a man got his hand cut off" points to an automatic tendency in her mind to think in ways that are catastrophic.

While her responses on the Rorschach test are also consistent with someone of limited intelligence (e.g., high percentage of simple animal responses, barely any responses seen with any movement, etc.), there are no indications of a thought disorder. In fact, there are no indications of schizophrenic condensation or psychotic thinking on any of the tests. What is more, there are not even indications of the kind of affect dominated thinking or displacement on the unstructured inkblots to substantiate a diagnosis of borderline ego pathology. She gives nineteen responses, of which 85 percent are commonly seen areas, and overall sees 74 percent of the responses without the intrusion of color, shading, or the blackness of the inkblots. In other words, there was a reasonable freedom from conflict in her responses, and her overall perceptual accuracy was 89 percent, which speaks to a very good sense of external reality in unstructured situations. 21 percent of her responses are popular, which indicates a good ability to see the commonplace, and there are no bizarre responses anywhere that would point to psychotic processes.

The freedom from conflict on her Rorschach responses is best understood as a combination of simple, concrete perceptions and massive denial of painful, anxiety-provoking, depressive, or aggressive affect. At one point, she even spontaneously comments, "the red does not look like anything." This kind of active rejection of the color is diagnostic of individuals who are prone to denial of things that stir emotion, and who are prone to impulsivity and action rather than experiencing their feelings as emotions. Certainly her cognitive limitations make it challenging to think about her feelings, as they are abstract, not tangible, only making it "easier" for her not to deal with her own narcissistic fragility, her hunger to be loved and admired, and her anger over multiple developmental interferences.

Considering her limitations and psychodynamics, in combination with her tendency to defy and sabotage those evaluating and treating her, it is understandable that she presents as potentially more psychiatrically disturbed than is the case. Diagnostically, however, this young woman is best understood as suffering from multiple developmental interferences, with very low intellectual capacities and severe narcissistic damage, all of which combined to make it very difficult for her to recognize and organize her emotional inner world. She struggles to deny and avoid a severe anaclitic depression with feelings of helplessness, confusion, and being lost (e.g., to one TAT card she says, "this is someone trapped in a black room . . . scared and confused"). She then says she has felt that way and barricaded herself in her room, just because she felt overwhelmed. Because she cannot soothe herself, she turns to alcohol and marijuana, the latter only further diminishing her intellectual capacities and motivation. Promiscuity is a way to feel admired and special, though she herself realizes that she often ends up hurt when she is discarded. Given the several TAT responses of loss, one of which she connected to the death of someone significant to her, it seems like this loss has not been grieved, yet another instance of her being unable to use her feelings as meaningful signals and work them through. In fact, her emotions confuse her, like her response to a TAT card of, "she is confused, sad, and scared . . . someone died . . . no . . . she is happy about something."

With so much emotional confusion, she has very limited frustration tolerance, and as a result is impulsive and action oriented. Whether loving feelings or aggressive ones, her emotions are more the boss of her than she is in charge of them. She is prone to express anger in self-defeating ways, like not cooperating with people who are trying to help her (e.g., to one TAT card showing a boy looking at a violin she says, "he's bored . . . so he'll probably play crappy"). Her self-image is very negative, including her body image (e.g., she defines the word "enormous" as meaning "fat" and then comments on being fat herself). Still, she is mostly caught up in the avoidance, denial, and acting out of her feelings than she is able to realize what they are.

From a treatment standpoint, she clearly needs the support of someone with greater intellectual capacities and empathy to help her put her feelings into words [Direct Support]. This relationship will take time to build trust, and she will likely need the external structure and support of an assisted-living situation if she is to remain stable during the psychotherapy. Given her cognitive limitations, she will need a lot of help putting things into words (i.e., mentalizing) so she can think about them. Her memory is not very efficient, so it is likely there will need to be repetition and simplicity, working on one issue at a time, helping her to prioritize.

Since she is acutely sensitive to narcissistic injury, the treatment process will be challenging. Progress will depend on building a sense of trust, and an atmosphere where she feels safely respected by those around her. She knows that she has a problem with her mood changes, so if she feels safe, she will presumably be open to experiencing and exploring better ways of dealing with her feelings, especially anger, which she can express in self-defeating ways like sabotaging her own treatment [Catharsis and some Insight]. It will be important to point this out to her, as it is likely to occur at times. She should benefit from advice, and if she likes her therapist she will be able to internalize the therapist's voice and better judgment [Introjection]. Her alcohol and drug abuse are likely to continue to be a problem, as will be men who wish to take advantage of her, so she will continue to need external support and structure if she is to make progress in these areas. Again, the treatment will need to be very concrete in making specific, simple coping strategies [Direct Support] that are repeated [working through].

She clearly has a soft spot in her heart for animals, and she wants to find employment in working with animals. This should be aggressively pursued, with an eye to work that will not place too much demand on her intellectually or emotionally [Direct Support]. She showed a very warm, loving side when she thought of animals, so she should be capable of great caring, especially since she feels safely loved by animals. While there are no indications on the tests of any severe psychopathology like a thought disorder, psychosis, or even borderline ego pathology, it will be important to keep in mind that she is very challenged narcissistically and intellectually, both of which have made it impossible for her to form any stable sense of identity, other than some sense of herself in relation to animals.

Example 4

The young adolescent girl was referred for psychological testing consultation to determine if her personality is organized on a neurotic or borderline level, and to what extent she is capable of distinguishing fantasy from reality. There is question that she may have a variation of Asperger's Syndrome, so it is hoped that the testing can determine if her object relations are sufficiently arrested to be consistent with this more severe diagnosis. In addition, this consultation was requested to determine her ego strengths, possible treatment recommendations for psychotherapy, the question of an underlying affective disorder that might be responsive to medications, and the extent to which it may be best for her to stay in a small, structured, private school environment.

Diagnostic Understanding: She struggles with such profound narcissistic vulnerability and rage that from early on in the testing session she acted as if the evaluation was an unreasonable and invalid assessment of her. Despite these reactions, she responded sufficiently that the results do allow for some valid conclusions. During the testing session, she relied on several interpersonal approaches to avoid direct experiences of her own narcissistic distress, at times challenging me and making me out to be unfair, at other times devaluing the tests themselves. For example, at one point she said, "You probably don't want these smart aleck answers." At another point she worried that if she gave inaccurate answers she would end up with a disgraceful label of "ADD" or "Bipolar" like "all the other kids" at her school. At moments in the testing when the prospect of failure loomed larger than she could tolerate, she tended to stop trying, often blaming the tests for being unfair rather than experiencing her difficulties as originating from within herself, and even though she said, "I like to be the best at things" several times during the testing, she could not observe the imposing, ideal version of herself that makes her capacity to tolerate depressive feelings so limited.

Despite these narcissistic struggles, from the standpoint of the psychological tests there is sufficient evidence of her having developed an inner world of "object relations" to rule out a diagnosis of Asperger's Syndrome, with its basis in a severe developmental arrest. She produces a good human "M" movement response on the Rorschach and her TAT stories reflect a lively inner world; also, Comprehension is one of her highest subtests on the WISC-R. Furthermore, her relationship with me during the testing was quite connected, showing a clear understanding and capacity for socially appropriate behaviors (even if at times she acted otherwise), and confirming that she can indeed form reciprocal, emotional attachments to others. Thus, the diagnosis of Asperger's Syndrome does not seem warranted, even though her action orientation, her hunger for attention, and her preoccupation with activities that make her feel worthwhile can produce Asperger's-like behaviors.

Nonetheless, her lack of observing ego, evidence of primitive idealizations, avoidance, denial, and provocative instances of projective identification, to say nothing of her history of acting out promiscuous behaviors, all point to a diagnosis of borderline ego structure. Her TAT stories are filled with aggressive and sexually dominated themes of food, marital betrayal, murder, and rape, yet when asked if *her own* stories might relate to herself or her own life, she comments that they are just "random stories." Similarly, on the Rorschach test she sees a knife, which quickly triggers her next response of "bruises and blood." On the positive side, there are no instances of serious lapses in her capacity for reality testing under structured conditions like the WISC-R; hence, there are no manifest indications on the tests of active psychotic processes. However, when faced with unstructured conditions like the Rorschach test, it is clear that her affects are not well integrated with cognitive processes. As a result, she is prone to act out her needs, wishes, and feelings rather that representing them symbolically in words, and her current capacity to think about and verbalize her affects is quite limited.

Considering the observations thus far, it's not surprising that her cooperation during the WISC-R test of her cognitive functioning was limited by her need to control and avoid challenges to her fragile narcissistic stability. In fact, her actual performance on the WISC-R may be as much as 20 percent less efficient than her potential. This conclusion is based on the fact that her Information, Similarities, and Comprehension scaled scores, the subtests that are most correlated with overall IQ scores, are higher than her remaining subtest scores. It is also based on the direct observation of her improved performance on those subsets where she seemed less affected by the prospect of failure.

Her tendency to quit rather than guess and her general avoidance of effort when she fears failure certainly lowered her scores. With this in mind, her WISC-R scores placed her in the Average range or the 24th to 37th percentile (Full Scale IQ of 89-95, Verbal IQ of 100-106, Performance IQ of 89-95). Her Comprehension scaled score was 12, whereas Picture Arrangement was 7, a significant difference that points to her having a greater cognitive understanding of the world around her than she can successfully utilize to guide her in her actions. Her lowest and most striking subtest score was a 4 on Picture Completion. Instead of seeing what was missing, she was repeatedly drawn to notice what looked flawed to her, in the same way she struggles with views of herself as defective. In other words, her narcissistic sensitivities cause her to miss what is most important in situations, and instead to focus on what she views as imperfections. With so much focus on defects, at times all she can do to avoid feeling worthless is to devalue others and focus on their imperfections.

Her memory as measured by the Babcock Story Recall Test of immediate and delayed recall also demonstrated a considerable lack of efficiency, well below what would be expected for her general cognitive abilities. Again, however, it is likely that this evaluation of her memory stirred up sufficient test anxiety, which added to her defensively motivated half-hearted approach and significantly reduced her potential for recollection. In fact, she was only able to remember 33 percent of the story on immediate recall and 43 percent of the story on delayed recall, both of which are lower than would be expected at the level of her overall intellectual capacities. But even though she has a higher cognitive potential, it is important to keep in mind that her actual intellectual abilities will in all likelihood function at the lower level of this testing under conditions that threaten her fragile narcissistic equilibrium.

Her tendency to act rather than think is also due to the global, overwhelming experience she has of sexual, angry, depressive, and anxious feelings. Because such feelings are too peremptory to tolerate, avoidance or expression is likely. Her sexual desires are connected to wanting to feel special, important, and desirable, in an effort to fend off feeling worthless, defective, and unlovable. Her body is central to these narcissistic struggles, in part due to normal adolescent development, but also due to a fixation she has with her body, including the idea that her lips are too large. Several test responses pointed to this preoccupation, and when I asked her about it she said kids always used to make fun of her big lips. Alongside such negative feelings about her body, however, her body also elicits sexual responses from boys, providing her with a way to feel wanted and important. Since she is inclined to developmentally immature idealizations or devaluation of others, and her sexuality is more about feeling desirable than gratifying her own desires, her promiscuity and her interest in older boys (or young men) are understandable.

Conclusions: Considering this girl's propensity to action over thought, she is clearly safer in a more structured school environment, with a small student-to-teacher ratio, and more adult supervision [Direct Support]. Her continued acting-out will be much harder to monitor and control at a large school. At the same time, being in a less competitive academic ambiance will help her, even though there is a downside in that she will be prone to devalue the idea of a "special school." For this reason, it will be important to get her tendency to devalue the school out in the open and to help her see how this is just one example of her overall narcissistic instability [Insight]. In this way, it will be possible to help her see how insecure she is about herself and how much her behavior is driven by efforts to feel worthwhile and desirable.

In other words, rather than thinking of her as depressed, her behaviors are better understood as efforts to avoid experiencing a potential for experiencing depressive feelings of emptiness and worthlessness that are intolerable. It is possible that some anti-depressant medications may provide a buffer that reduces her potential exposure to depression, thereby providing her with some relief from the degree of ever-present threat of narcissistic mortification and giving her more capacity to control her behaviors [Direct Support]. At the same time, such relief should also increase her capacity for working in psychotherapy; in particular, efforts to help her consciously appreciate the ways in which she feels worthless (e.g., her devalued view of her own body), and the ways in which she avoids feeling depressed. Only by realizing that her sexuality is mostly driven by wanting attention in order to feel lovable and desirable will she be able to understand that her promiscuity can never be a foundation of resilient esteem, or of an identity based on her talents and interests [Insight].

Fortunately, the same hunger for relationships that underlies her problems is also a potential source of building a treatment alliance. In order for this to happen, she needs a therapist who can steer clear of trying to control her behavior, and instead strive to understand how she feels from her point of view. Only by first establishing such empathy connections will it be possible to help her understand the underlying needs that drive her behaviors. This will require continual interpretations of her projected criticisms and devaluation [Insight]. Also, it will require forbearance in the face of her provocations, as she can evoke counter-transference feelings of being useless, uncaring, and incompetent. It is important that the therapist endeavor not to identify with these provocations, not to react negatively or defensively to feeling devalued. For when the therapist offers a more benign experience of the interaction, by understanding the true nature of these provocations, by not taking them personally, she can take in this more benign experience of the relationship [Introjection and Identification].

She needs but will find it difficult to tolerate at least a twice-weekly exploratory psychotherapy, in addition to all the supportive measures in her life that aim to help her control her behaviors. It should be anticipated that treatment takes time, the time needed to slowly make changes in her life [Working Through]. As she gets more in touch with her underlying depressive core, with both anaclitic feelings of helplessness and introjective struggles with feeling worthless, it will be important to help her anticipate [Insight] and monitor [Direct Support] both her potential for suicidal behaviors and the possibility that she might act out her needs in a fantasy connected with teenage pregnancy. Should her behaviors become more out of control and dangerous despite outpatient treatment efforts, it may be important to consider residential treatment at some point in the future [Direct Support].

Example 5

Diagnostic Understanding: While this mid-adolescent boy, referred to get a better understanding of his failure to thrive both academically and socially, was clearly somewhat cautious in his responsiveness to the psychological tests, he did make a sincere effort. As a result, the test results do reveal the psychological nature of his difficulties. There is considerable evidence of intra-psychic deficits, cognitive regression, and conflicts that are in all likelihood causing him to retreat from the real world into the fantasy world of a virtual computer game. While there is not conclusive evidence of a formal schizophrenic thought disorder, there are numerous instances of a striking loosening of associative thought processes. For example, on the Babcock Story Recall Test he remembers *10 miles from Albany* as being "10 miles from agony [sic]."

His thinking is confused and concrete as well, pointing to marked cognitive regression. On the WAIS-R, for example, when asked in what direction the sun rises, he says, "from bottom to top." When asked to name four U.S. presidents since 1950, he names "the two Bushes, Lincoln, and Washington." When asked how many months in a year he first says thirteen and changes it to twelve. He sees pliers as looking like a wrench and a violin as looking like a guitar. He says dogs and lions are alike in that "they both have the same shapes." He says that compassion means "to have someone with you" (i.e., he seems to associate to the word companion based on alliteration). When asked how *praise* and *punishment* are alike he says, "praise is like praying." In other words, the meanings of words with similar sounds are confused; past and present are confused; words associated with things are confused; and overall his thinking has become very concrete and literal. While there are no instances of any florid schizophrenic condensation of thought on the tests, clearly his cognitive processes are slipping.

Given so much confusion in his thought processes, it is not surprising that he is confused about how to deal with the real world. For example, when asked what he would do if he *found an envelope on the street that was sealed, addressed, and had a new stamp,* he replied, "most people would just leave it on the ground." In other words, he both demonstrates and denies his passivity and indecision about what to do (i.e., "most people"). When asked how he *would find his way out of the forest were he lost in the daytime,* he says, "I'd need to be there to see what I could do," again denying his helplessness. Clearly he is struggling to avoid feelings of helplessness and being lost.

On the WAIS-R standardized scores, the extent of his confusion and cognitive regression became all too apparent. He seemed to be making a real effort to do well; yet he scored overall at the bottom 8th percentile ranking for his age (Full Scale IQ of 76-82; Verbal IQ of 79-85; Performance IQ of 73-83). Because the sophistication of his projective test responses is not consistent with such limited intelligence, it seems most likely this is a cognitive regression. His memory as measured by the Babcock Story Recall Test is similarly limited, as he can only recall a little more than half the story on both immediate and delayed recall. His highest subtest score was on Digit Span, a measure of immediate recall of random numbers, speaking to adequate concentration as long as the circumstances are very detached from any emotional meaning or conflict.

His ego struggles to keep a firm hold on external reality, for even though his Rorschach responses were guarded and limited to one for each card, only one-third of his responses seen based on their form were accurate resemblances of the inkblots, whereas a minimum two-thirds is the norm. This is an indicator of a relative lack of conflict-free ego resources. On the other hand, when some emotion and fantasy are a part of his inkblot responses, his perceptual accuracy improves. This finding is counter-intuitive (typically, affect, fantasy, and conflict lower perceptual accuracy, as intra-psychic factors influence external perceptions). This paradoxical finding suggests that his ego may use some fantasy, emotion, and conflict to enhance his hold on external reality. Such a pattern of Rorschach test responses can predict some cases where individuals use depressive affect to enhance their grasp on external reality; as a result, they can react to anti-depressant medications with decreased reality testing, whereas anti-anxiety medications may have a positive effect on their ego functioning.

70 percent of his responses are to the whole inkblot rather than part of it, again typical of a young child, and only one response involves human percepts, indicative of a very limited inner world of object relations, as do his TAT stories, which are also very limited in complexity. The contrast between such serious ego regression and his blithe attitude toward his problems is an effort to avoid the narcissistic mortification of a full-on encounter with the severity of his ego deficits. His TAT stories are filled with themes of death, loss, and helplessness, but it is too overwhelming for him to consciously face at this time, so he denies any significant relationship between these stories and his own life. Nonetheless, on the more structured tests like the WAIS-R, it was apparent that he became more agitated as his cognitive impairments were exposed. It is likely he struggles with such anxiety at school too, so he falls back on avoidance and denial. Facing reality is too great a threat to his fragile esteem and sense of self, so he retreats more and more to a world where he can experience ego mastery, even though it is regressive and grandiose. His last Rorschach response, which reminded him of a throne akin to one in his computer game, points to the increasing importance this retreat holds for him.

Conclusions: It is clear that his cognitive ego functioning is seriously impaired, and while not yet fully indicative of a formal schizophrenic thought disorder, it may be headed in that direction. It is possible that he is moving more in the direction of a schizoid or schizotypal personality disorder, but based on the test results, he does not appear simply depressed with a learning disability. It will be important to monitor the progression of his symptoms closely in order to follow any further regression in his cognitive processes, as such regression would cause increasing confusion about reality, and emergence of psychotic anxieties that could require changes in medication [Direct Support].

In order to promote as much academic leaning as possible, while at the same time respecting his psychological deficits, he would do best in a school environment for adolescents with serious psychiatric problems [Direct Support]. It is not in his best interest to permit too much isolation and retreat, as he will develop less and less social anxiety tolerance over time [Working Through]. He clearly needs ongoing supportive psychotherapy [Direct Support], with exploratory and insight related components if and when feasible and tolerable. Where medications are concerned, it will be important to monitor the possibility that his ego uses depressive affects to improve his grasp on external reality; less anti-depressant medications potentially contribute to the extent of his ego regression. With so much cognitive regression, anxiety is likely to be as much if not more of a problem than depression.

Example 6

Diagnostic Understanding: This young, adult man was referred for psychological testing in order to explore the underlying reasons for his failure to thrive, including the possibility he has very limited cognitive capacities. At first, when asked, this man said he had "no idea" why the psychological testing was being done, but when asked more specific questions it was clear he did have ideas; he just tended to be so passive that his first reaction was to assume he did not know. Although this young man complains of having an attention deficit disorder, and indeed he does have difficulty staying focused and completing academic tasks, his cognitive functioning on the WAIS-R never falls below average on any of the subtests. Overall, he scores in the High-Average range or the 81st-90th percentile (Full Scale IQ of 113-119, Verbal IQ of 113-119, Performance IQ of 108-116). The Digit Span subtest of attention is one of his highest scores, with recall of eleven numbers forward and twelve numbers backward. He had no difficulty doing arithmetic calculations in his head, another indication of his ability to concentrate, and while his memory on the Babcock Story Recall Test was marginal, when pressed for more recollection he did remember more of the story, suggesting a problem of motivation more than a primary cognitive deficit. His cognitive functioning on the sensori-motor performance subsets of the WAIS-R was also quite adequate, and the lack of a significant discrepancy between his Verbal and Performance subtest scores further suggests he does not have a distinct, primary cognitive dysfunction like an attention deficit disorder. He had plenty of energy for the Performance subtests, so there is no evidence on the WAIS-R for cognitive slowing secondary to depression, nor did symptoms of anxiety encumber his thinking. Thus, on the tests his difficulties do not emerge as being primarily caused by cognitive impairments.

There are no indications on the tests of severe, underlying psychopathology in the form of a thought disorder or any psychotic processes. Under both structured conditions like the WAIS-R and unstructured conditions like the projective tests, he maintains adequate reality sense and reasonable judgment with few exceptions, and demonstrates an intact reality-fantasy boundary. Thus, his failure to thrive does not appear to be symptomatic of any underlying, grave psychological illness that is threatening to surface. At the same time, he did give only limited projective test responses, so it is possible more severe psychopathology was concealed by his avoidance of much immersion in the tests.

Taking his responses as is, however, his emotional immaturity and his overall passivity are striking. When he does not immediately know the answer to an item on the WAIS-R he quickly gives up without much concern or effort; but if he is good at a task right away he works at it and can do quite well. Thus, he seems to lack inner sources of motivation to aspire and persevere. On the Rorschach Test, he only gives a paltry eight responses, with no responses at all to four of the ten inkblots. In general, he is indifferent when he cannot come up with a response, and the responses he does give are easily seen and more typical of a young child whose inner world is developmentally unsophisticated.

On the TAT, his stories reflect a predominance of anaclitic object relations, where the characters are mostly reliant on each other in dependent ways. People are either propping each other up, looking to each other for stability, or helplessly alone. Even on the WAIS-R these anaclitic dynamics play out. For example, on the Picture Completion item where a pitcher is tipped and one is to notice the water is not pouring, he says there is no one holding up the pitcher. On the Arithmetic subtest, he wants paper right away rather than doing the problems in his head (which he then is able to do). When asked the Comprehension question about what he would do were he to see fire at the movies he says, "yell fire and run . . . or run and then yell fire," demonstrating his passivity in the face of his own emotions and a narcissistic orientation.

Diagnostically, this man is struggling with a mixed personality disorder with dependent and narcissistic features, leaving him vulnerable to the feelings of emptiness and helplessness associated with an anaclitic depression. His descriptions of his parents as lost, aimless people tell the story. To whatever extent these are or are not accurate descriptions of his actual parents, they are the parents constructed in his own mind, leaving him without inner sources of direction, aspirations, and motivation.

Conclusions: This man, who is in fact quite lost and lacks mature, inner psychological resources, needs an intensive but structured psychotherapy that can help him explore and understand the developmental underpinnings of his failure to thrive, as well as helping him develop a plan for his future [Direct Support and Insight]. At the same time, he needs a therapeutic relationship that can begin to provide a basis for more healthy identifications as he struggles to find himself [Identification]. This means a relationship with someone who comes to matter to him, and someone whom he feels really cares about him.

Since he cannot go back in time and re-do his childhood, he will need support and encouragement to take on life challenges. Truly he needs to "build character" by forcing himself into situations where he can develop a greater sense of pride and purpose. Avoidance is the enemy here, and he all too easily gives up, blaming external factors or internal deficits that are beyond his control. He will clearly need a lot of structure in the therapy until he is capable of providing it for himself, but it would be best if the structure aimed to get him started but then left him to develop his own resources, lest he use the therapy as another anaclitic relationship. This model would best apply to the work in the treatment as well as his efforts outside it [Working Through]. Most important will be the establishment of a relationship to his therapist that has emotional importance to him. One final caveat: given his limited responsiveness on the projective tests, it will be important to continue to monitor for the unlikely possibility of some more pernicious underlying psychopathology.

Example 7

Diagnostic Understanding: The extent to which this young man's severe depression and despair are manifest on the psychological tests is alarming. While he is highly intelligent, his scores on the Performance subtests of the WAIS-R are 46 points lower than on the Verbal subtests. This is a huge, extremely significant difference (Full Scale IQ of 119-125 or 90th to 95th percentile, Verbal IQ of 137-143, Performance IQ of 90-98). Because he is capable of doing the visual-perceptual-motor tasks, the difference is not evidence of an inability; he is just very slowed by the depression and consequently loses credit on all the Performance timed subtests. Consistent with this finding, his two lowest Verbal subtests are measures of attention and concentration (Digit Span and Arithmetic), which are also cognitive impairments that are symptomatic of depression. The fact that he can still perform well on the Babcock Story Recall Test of memory, both immediate and delayed, is evidence of his highly superior intellect.

Given the fact that the great discrepancy between his Verbal and Performance IQs is mostly due to slowed performance, and the clear evidence of severe depression on the projective tests, his cognitive deficits on the WAIS-R are not probable signs of neuropsychological impairment. Furthermore, on the Bender-Gestalt test, his lack of energy and motivation is evident in a hasty approach to the drawings, but all the designs are done correctly, with no rotations or other signs of cognitive impairment. In fact, despite his haste he completes some of the more difficult Bender-Gestalt designs with remarkable accuracy. In other words, there are no indications on these tests that would point to neuropsychological impairment.

On the other hand, the extent to which his mind lacks freedom from conflict is alarming. On the Rorschach test, for example, only 38 percent of his sixteen responses are seen in a neutral, conflict-free manner, whereas twice that percentage is the desired minimum. While he can maintain a good hold on reality as long as affects are isolated or intellectualized, at times his excessive reliance on intellectualization can lead to somewhat odd thinking. For example, he defined the word *domestic* as meaning, "encompassed in a sphere close to oneself." When affects do break through, however, the result is regression, confusion, a potential for impulsivity, and feeling overwhelmed. As a result, his depression has a significant anaclitic component and is partly intolerable because it brings intense feelings of helplessness, emptiness, and agitation. Thus, it is not surprising that he turns to alcohol and drugs as a form of self-medication.

Because he is extremely intelligent, he can at times appear to have more developmentally advanced ego structure than is the case. Accordingly, he gives some very mature, complex responses on the Rorschach test, even ones that show some capacity to intellectually organize aggression. Also, he maintains good reality orientation on the structured tests like the WAIS-R. A very different picture emerges, however, when he responds to the unstructured, chromatic Rorschach cards, known to stir more intense affect than the achromatic cards. These responses betray a potential for perceptions determined by his feelings, a disorganizing intrusion of aggression, a loss of reality sense as his efforts to intellectualize fail, and a global shift to seeing things as deteriorating. For example, to the last Rorschach card, he says, "it's the birth canal . . . rotting . . . infected . . . attacked by various outside organisms. There are two fertilized eggs trying to make their way to the outside of the birth canal, but the canal is decomposing everything." He goes on to say so many colors are opposing forces; the eggs are full of life but everything else is death and destruction. Given his detachment, it is not surprising that he can maintain equanimity while reporting a response so filled with deterioration and rage.

Such developmentally immature, emotionally dominated perceptions on the unstructured tests, accompanied by a good reality orientation on the structured tests, are diagnostic of borderline personality structure, in his case accompanied by depressive and addictive features. Consistent with this diagnostic impression, there are numerous indications on the tests of developmentally immature idealizations and identity diffusion, which is related to the impossibility of integrating such ideals with his exceptional albeit real capabilities. His perfectionism is painful to observe. For example, he made one error on an Arithmetic question early on in the three-hour testing session, and continued to be troubled by the error for the remainder of the session. When I commented on it continuing to bother him, he said, "oh . . . this is going to bother me for days." Sadly, I believed him.

Having an inner world so "populated" by developmentally immature ideals and struggling to maintain so much emotional detachment leaves him without inner resources for pride and narcissistic regulation. He truly does not know who he is or where he is going. As a result, he is vulnerable to latching onto some external source of identity, purpose, and meaning, but it is unlikely any of them will take. His TAT stories portray a man who is in utter despair, who feels intense self-loathing, who has no relationships that feel secure, and who has given up on life. The people in his projective stories are tragic, depressed, isolated, lost, unloved, trapped in darkness, running out of time; and he identifies with all of them. It was apparent as he looked at the TAT cards that the stories were bringing more of his despair to the surface. Being so utterly lost, there are not surprisingly oblique references to regressive, passive-dependent wishes on the tests, but they are for the most part unconscious due to the threat of narcissistic mortification such wishes bring with them. He may not be adapting to the developmental challenges of growing up, but being a needy, dependent little boy is unbearably humiliating.

Conclusions: Clearly this young man is in grave danger and needs immediate treatment. The possibility of his making more desperate attempts to reduce his agitated despair is real and could be lethal. A medication regimen that will reduce his exposure to intolerable, agitated depressive feelings could provide him with the most immediate relief, but given his addictive traits, it will be important to find medications that do not have addictive properties. Until he is more stabilized in a psychotherapy relationship, regulating prescriptions to avoid lethal doses should be considered, along with ways to make certain he is complying with the medication regimen [Direct Support].

As soon as possible, he should begin to establish a supportive psychotherapy relationship, face-to-face, at least three times a week, with the idea of introducing more and more exploratory interventions as the treatment alliance and medication provide him with stability [Direct Support and Insight]. He is extremely intelligent and verbal, so he possesses the cognitive capacities to appreciate the nature of his inner world, and he might benefit from the more realistic perceptions that could come from more cognitive-behavioral interventions [Introjection and Insight], but he will also need a therapist he can use as a developmental object, someone who will help him forge an identity, a sense of his own abilities, desires, talents, wishes, values, and preferences. In this sense, a male therapist will be a more suitable role model for him [Introjection and Identification]. Over time, as he applies the discoveries and the other positive effects of his treatment [Working Through], it will hopefully transition to a more exploratory psychotherapy. Eventually, he might even be a candidate for analysis, which could hold the greatest potential for his development.

In these examples I have tried to show how careful, penetrating diagnoses of patients can reveal which of the six basic modes of therapeutic action are more or less likely to be successfully therapeutic for a particular patient. With this information it is possible to choose an approach to treatment that emphasizes those particular modes of therapeutic action. In the next chapter, I will illustrate the actual employment of the basic modes of therapeutic action over the course of an exploratory, psychoanalytic treatment.

FOUR

Individual Treatment Illustration

This clinical depiction of the first year of an intensive, exploratory, two-year psychotherapy with a mid-adolescent girl is intended to demonstrate how during treatment the different modalities of therapeutic action are manifest over the course of the actual process of the therapy. In fact, it is an account that draws from the treatment of several teenagers and from my supervision of teenagers not in treatment with me, so in the end it is a kind of reality-based fiction. I use an actual name for the patient, although Mary is not her real name, as I find referring to people as M. or using aliases is artificial and detracts from the reader's ability to experience the therapy as an interaction between two real people. Suffice it to say that all names and potentially identifying information are deeply disguised, making it impossible to differentiate this treatment from the kind of symptoms and conflicts that are the case for many, many teenage girls. Despite such essential efforts to protect the confidentiality of all patients, I believe the clinical narrative conveys a process that reveals the evolving role of the six modes of therapeutic action as a treatment progresses.

As with the previous chapter on diagnoses, I will insert in [brackets] the primary forms of therapeutic action where indicated as they emerge. Again, however, it is important to keep in mind that I will not refer to all modes of therapeutic action, only the primary one(s), and that it is usually the case in reality that several modes will be in effect, to various degrees, at any point in the treatment process. That being said, there are several considerations I want to highlight. First, it will become apparent that utilizing various modes of therapeutic action is as much a part of the assessment, evaluation, and the initial sessions of the treatment as of the middle of the treatment process itself. Second, there is no specific order in which various modes of therapeutic action are employed. And finally, the utilization of therapeutic actions in this treatment is individualized, conforming to the process of the treatment as it unfolds rather than being decided beforehand; this approach is quite different from contemporary forms of "manualized treatments," where the patient follows a pre-programmed treatment plan, with pre-determined therapeutic actions and techniques.

INITIAL PATIENT CONTACT AND ASSESSMENT

Mary's mother called me wanting a consultation for her mid-adolescent daughter. She was concerned about the increasing adversarial tone to their relationship. She also wondered if treatment might benefit her daughter during the "difficult" teenage years. I had several initial meetings with Mary and her mom, both together and individually. From these meetings it became clear that mom agreed with her daughter that she herself is anxious and overprotective. With Mary driving and wanting more freedom, her mom's anxieties were an increasing source of conflict between them. Mary also agreed that she has temper outbursts with her mom that are not an effective means of communication, and she expressed a desire for help to find better ways to deal with these conflicts.

Over the course of the evaluation several other significant concerns came to light. Mary was struggling with failing grades, which she admitted was because she wasn't putting much time into her studies. She said she preferred her social life to homework; specifically, spending more time with her boyfriend and being with several of her girlfriends. She said that while the work is not as hard at her current school, she's still worried that not wanting to study will eventually cause her grades to slip. She worried poor grades would make it hard to get into a good four-year-college. I asked if she'd ever tried to figure out why she didn't want to study. At first, she talked about the problem as just being the way everybody feels. I said, "but I bet you have friends who study, even though they may not want to . . . yet it seems to be so much harder for you." She agreed and said she'd never thought much about it, but maybe her aversion to studying did have to do with some underlying problem [beginning of Insight]. She added that she was interested in trying to figure out what might be causing this school problem.

Mary also acknowledged having a very low opinion of herself, especially when it came to her looks. She continued to see herself as overweight and unattractive, despite the fact that she'd lost most of the extra weight and that others now tell her she is good looking. Again, she talked about this as a matter of fact, without any curiosity. I pointed out that losing the weight did not seem to change her view of herself. She was intrigued and thought that there must be more reasons for her negative view of herself [more Insight]. She told me she was aware her insecurities limit her potential (e.g., she likes to dance, she is quite good at it, but is too self-conscious to dance in public, even though she would love to be a dancer). I told her that it seemed this was another problem we could try to understand.

Another area of concern in my mind during the evaluation was her complete denial that growing up in a family with many siblings had affected her, or held any meaning for her or any significance in her life at all. Similarly, she seemed to avoid thinking about her father tending to be distant and mostly working. It soon became clear in talking with her that she just avoided thinking about such issues. Her mother was also concerned about Mary dating a considerably older boy. Mary didn't see this as a problem either, and just thought of it as another example of her mother's tendency to overreact. Nonetheless, I pointed out that the relationship with this boy was another source of conflict with her mom, and she agreed that made it a problem.

DIAGNOSTIC AND PSYCHODYNAMIC UNDERSTANDING

Initially, Mary's symptoms pointed to a descriptive, DSM IV diagnosis of dysthymic disorder with some features of an oppositional defiance disorder. Beginning with her pre-adolescent years, Mary's self-esteem had been dropping. She said she was pudgy as a younger child, and while that's been less problematic since she became a teenager, she still focuses on aspects of her physical appearance that bother her. She also tends to undervalue her talents, like her intelligence and her dancing ability, and while she knows others feel she is special, she does not feel that way about herself. In school, she's lacked the energy and concentration for her studies, and finds it increasingly more difficult to maintain an interest in academics. Her difficulties with staying on task were specific to doing schoolwork at home, and she did not meet the criteria for an attention deficit disorder. When I first saw her, these depressive symptoms had been going on long enough to be considered chronic. It also seemed that her adolescent development was not progressing to increasing independence and autonomy.

Her history, her current life, and her approach to the evaluation with me all demonstrated that she had many strengths and overall a neurotic ego structure. She had a good sense of the boundary between reality and fantasy; there were no indications of problems with affect-dominated thinking and she had good impulse control. Her capable past performance at an academically demanding school indicated that she possessed good cognitive abilities, and her history of stable, significant attachments, both with family and friends, demonstrated a developmentally appropriate capacity for object relations.

Dynamically, there were several important considerations relevant to understanding her depression. For one, she had considerable capacity to compartmentalize and deny certain realities of her life. This permitted considerable isolation of affect to a point where she did not consciously experience emotional distress. For example, she claimed that having many siblings did not hold any importance to her and that she had no feelings about it. Similarly, she "seemed" to have no feelings about the fact that her father was largely out of the picture at home. Even though her family has quietly accepted the reality of an absentee father, it seems likely that she has felt a "rejection" by him, which may have contributed to her devalued view of herself. Since she admitted she did not know her father very well, she was at risk for retaining developmentally immature idealizations that remained unchallenged by reality and corresponding ideal versions of herself that she could never satisfy, further contributing to her devalued view of herself. This formulation seemed borne out by her relationship to her current boyfriend, who was older and "teased" her about her insecurities, yet she continued to idealize him. While friends and family felt he was unkind to her and she could do much better, she did not see it this way at all.

In fact, her claims to independence, bolstered by her rebellion against her mother, hid the reality that she looked to others to make decisions for her. She recognized that it was very difficult if not impossible for her to maintain a truly independent stance, especially if someone disagreed with her. I reminded her that she had earlier described her mother in similar terms, and I pointed out the likeness. She was both surprised and distressed to see the similarity [Insight]. She went on to say that this tendency to give in to others is a problem, and she expressed a desire to change it.

Given Mary's stable ego organization, the evidence of her good intellectual capacities, and in light of the depressive symptoms that were currently interfering with her academic progress, I recommended intensive exploratory psychotherapy, both to Mary and her mother. I mentioned the tensions in her relationship with her mother, and her devalued view of herself. In my mind I also thought that she was showing indications of seeking neurotic attachments with boys, but I chose not to emphasize this given that Mary did not see it as a problem.

THE FIRST YEAR OF TREATMENT

During her first therapy hour she was on time, polite, and tended to be quiet, similar to the way she was with me during the evaluation. While we were working out a schedule of meeting three times weekly, she asked me why we would meet so often. She was outwardly satisfied with a general answer from me (e.g., "these are serious problems you've been having with school; we want to help the situation as soon as possible and understand what is going on"). She appeared grateful for the help, and she expressed no negative feelings about the time commitment. I felt relief, given that I'd had difficulty working out frequent meeting times with other adolescents, but it also crossed my mind that this was consistent with her passivity and compliance. We discussed the privacy of our sessions. I told her that I would not report anything to her parents, except when we met, which they would know because they were paying the bill. I explained the only exception would be if I thought she was in danger and they needed to do something to protect her. She imagined it would be hard for her anxious, overprotective mother to be "out of the loop." I pointed out how her mother's attitudes seemed to have a strong presence in her mind [Insight about Introjection].

I then invited her to talk about what was on her mind. Without much hesitation, she went on to tell me that she was grounded recently for coming home late. She did not tell her mother the whole truth, leaving out that she was late because she had secretly gone to see some boys. I wondered to myself if she was testing me; would I tell her mother this secret? I asked about her time with the boys, what they did together. She said they're just friends and they just "drove around" for a while, implying there was nothing sexual about it. She added that she wasn't planning to go, that she really did not want to go, but the two boys had persuaded her. I mentioned that it seemed like an example of how it can be hard for her to say "no" if it means disappointing people. She heartily agreed, adding that it is a big problem for her [Insight].

Over the next few sessions, in working out the times of our meetings, I was surprised that she expressed no preferences about when we met, and I said so. With some hesitation, she told me that she was agreeing to appointment times that really were not her preference. I added that it sounded like what happened with the two boys, when she went along despite her not wanting to go with them.

At first, she said nothing else to me. Later, she described having the idea that I was the one who should tell her when to come. Seeing me as the authority wasn't a question in her mind. She saw a similar pattern with her mother, but unlike with me, where her mother was concerned she added how much she "hates" her mother telling her what to do. She said this was one of the reasons she hates to study, with her mother routinely telling her she needs to study more. I told her that I did not sense she was angry with me, like she feels with her mother, even though she'd had a similar experience with me. She agreed she did not feel angry with me, rationalizing that I was just trying to work out the times for our meetings. She also said she doesn't like teachers who tell her what to do, and she wondered why she's recently been quietly not complying with bossy teachers. I pointed out her passivity in "quietly refusing to cooperate." She agreed and she spoke of an increasing awareness that she has a problem being assertive, but that she can see she has a way of quiet defiance [Insight].

Very early on in the treatment, her passivity and compliance were evident in her requests that I tell her what to talk about in the sessions. In the beginning, her difficulty talking spontaneously was so great that I did help her out [Direct Support], like when I casually said I had little sense of what her days were like. Then, with no hesitation she told me about her routine, including her procrastination with homework. When her mother told her to do her work she procrastinated even more. She didn't like one of her teachers because she was "too bossy." I said, "you clearly don't like some people telling you what to do, but it seems more complicated to me, because at other times you do want to be told, like wanting me to tell you what to talk about during our meetings." She said it was somehow different with me, but she didn't understand it.

Over the next month, her difficulty talking without some prompting from me continued, though it seemed more a difficulty getting started, as once she got going she had no difficulty filling the hours and telling me about herself. She had a job working at a restaurant. She'd saved some money because her mother forced her to put some money aside, which she both resented and appreciated, knowing that were it up to her she'd have already spent it all. She talked about having a boyfriend who was quite a bit older, and how that bothered her mother. She said she had a teasing relationship with him and they made fun of each other a lot.

Over time it emerged that she'd started many activities like soccer and cello, but she eventually quit them all. She blamed her mother and father for being weak and not "making" her see things through to completion. I asked if she and her mother were alike in this way. She said she knew they were and it bothered her. She said her mother often started projects, made plans, promised things would be done, and did not follow through. Soon she raised the subject of school, letting me know that she was now two months into her junior year, and she could tell she was already beginning to slack off. She was surprised when I *asked* her if she thought it was a problem, as she'd just assumed I would be like her mother and father, insisting that good grades and going to college were expected of her. This moment of surprise seemed to mark a deepening of the treatment alliance and a shift in her view of my authority. She was beginning to see me as more than just another parent, and she later reported that recalling such encounters with me led her to think more for herself [Introjection].

She told me about how she wanted to go to college and follow the family traditions. I asked her a few questions about things like PSATs, but it became very clear that she had little sense of what was involved in preparing for college applications. She thought she'd taken the PSATs, but her mother had lost the results, so she never had found out how she did; she added that her mother tended to be disorganized. She could ask her father but he was gone most of the time, adding it's more like she doesn't really have a father. I told her I was impressed at how much things that would bother others did not seem to bother her, like not having much of a father. She agreed she was good at pushing her feelings aside, but said it was also a problem. She doesn't really know how she feels about things a lot of the time. As this theme developed, it became apparent that she has difficulty making any decisions on her own, even deciding what food she will eat. In fact, she told me she often asks her friends and her boyfriend to order for her in restaurants.

As the treatment progressed, I learned how important others' opinions were to her. Also, that Mary used to be overweight and felt she was ugly. Now she had lost a lot of the extra weight, and she was even beginning to believe people's compliments. She complained that she did not get along with some of her siblings, and that at times she felt bullied by some of them. More emerged about her relationship with her boyfriend, having to do with their mistrust of each other. For example, he wants to check her cell phone for a record of possible calls from other guys. She continued to talk about not knowing what she really likes and said that her grades were slipping. I asked her to tell me more about her efforts to study, and it became clear to both of us that she did not study enough because she felt the need to be with friends and she couldn't tolerate being alone [Insight]. She said her worst fear was that her friends would do things without her; she'd be left out and others wouldn't think to include her anymore. She knew she was insecure and this fear was too much to be normal, but she couldn't stand being at home trying to study when she could be with friends. She also said she accepted anyone's help in learning how to study, so we spent some time discussing specific strategies for doing her studies, which she said she was able to implement, adding that it helped to hear my encouraging voice in her mind [Direct Support and Introjection].

During this time, several things happened between us. She and her mother mixed up an appointment time and she missed a session. She worried that I'd be upset with her and told me she'd gotten angry with her mother for forgetting. I replied, "it's interesting . . . you told me about being afraid to get angry with people, but with your mother it seems different." She agreed it was different, and thought she must feel more secure with her mother [Insight] to be able to get angry with her. She realized that she doesn't worry her mother will reject her. I mentioned that with me it seemed she was worried I'd reject her, so she worried I'd be angry when she'd forgotten our appointment. She agreed and said she really didn't know me that well.

By comparison, at the beginning of another session she came in very surprised that I had ordered a new magazine for the waiting room. When we started the therapy she had told me none of my magazines interested her—which surprised me given her passivity but did not surprise me given my magazines—so I ordered one that she said she likes [Direct Support]. The day the magazine arrived, she came in with it in hand saying: "No way you got this for me . . . my mother never remembers to do what she promises." While I acknowledged her surprise, and felt a positive development in our relationship, I also experienced some concern that by ordering the magazine I had enacted competitive wishes to be a better parent to her, a wish that was mixed in with and could compromise my desire to help her as her therapist.

At this point in our treatment, her father returned home from work travel for a longer time than was typical. She focused on feeling that he is selfish and bossy when he's around the house (e.g., she said, "we always have to watch what he wants on the TV"). By comparison, she continued to describe her mother as self-sacrificing, overprotective, and anxious. In one instance, for example, her mother sat for three hours in the car while Mary went into a teenage dance club; this because her mother was so worried it might not be safe to leave her there with her friends. Her grades were slipping to Bs and a C, and she even reported getting an F on a history examination. She wondered why she had been so afraid of teachers in the past, as she now thought, "what can they really do to me?" While she experienced this as becoming more independent, I wondered about her identifications with a new peer group, and therefore what in fact would be another instance of passivity. I made no comments at this point, however, thinking she might hear me as siding with her mother against her friends. I did have some concern that she seemed to be drifting toward a group of teenagers who were not college bound and who were not trying to succeed in high school. But going to college was my aspiration for her, her family's aspiration for her, not clearly what she had yet decided she wanted for herself.

At this point in the therapy, I noticed that she was coming in for the sessions and openly talking about a number of areas of her life including her family, school, boyfriend, friends, and interest in dancing. She wished for a career as a dancer, but worried it was impossible given her inhibitions and shyness. She told me she could dance well but not in front of people. She could dance in the school chorus because she blended in with everyone else. I asked her if she'd considered that we might try to understand her fears and perhaps she could get over them. She replied that she was interested but pessimistic because she could not imagine feeling confident in herself; as long as she could remember she'd always felt insecure.

More and more, I heard about struggles with her mother over her curfew times and where she'd go with her friends. This came to a head with her mother calling me after Mary had taken the car without permission and stayed out very late on a school night. In talking with Mary she knew she'd pushed the limit with her mother, she was willing to agree to more reasonable curfew times, but she said she just cannot work this out with her mother, as they just argue. I wondered how I might help, and after some sessions she was able to work out with me what she felt was an acceptable curfew [Direct Support]. With her mother, however, she tried but just could not work out a mutual arrangement. Despite the difficulty with her mother, she said she'd continue to try. I told her that I wondered if she said this to please me. She agreed that was probably true but she still needed to work things out with her mother.

As we moved into the fifth month of the therapy, her passive compliance became more thematic of our sessions and more in her awareness [Insight]. She described herself doing things primarily to keep others happy with her at work, with her boyfriend, with friends, and at home. As a result, she worked at times she didn't want to work, she drove her sister places she did not want to go, and she went to her boyfriend's when she'd rather he come to her house. She clearly recognized that her mother was the main person she could refuse. As was the case in the previous years, her inability to do her homework continued to result in failing grades. She wanted help with planning for college, and she described her family as expecting she would go.

She felt that she got mixed messages in that she was told college was important but no one took the time to help her. Indeed, as we discussed it she had no clue about the process of applying to college, about standardized college tests, about what colleges expect of applicants, or about the timing of the application process. Going to college was little more than an idea to her. The more we discussed college issues in the sessions [Direct Support], the more she seemed to take an interest outside the sessions [Identification]. She started to learn about SAT preparation courses and the timelines for applying. Also, she connected with her high school counselor and started to get information from him.

Finally she decided it would be a good idea to have a session with her mother to try to work out the curfew. We all met; I functioned as a kind of mediator [Direct Support], and they compromised on reasonable times for weeknights and a later time for weekends. While they were both surprised they could reach an agreement, I was distracted by the thought that these curfews were later than I would accept for my children, again tipping me off to my own paternalistic feelings that were mixed in with the treatment. While it appeared that in many ways I was functioning as a developmental object, the challenge was to be available for Mary to use me without my enacting the role of being a parent with her. I realized that her passivity tended to pull me toward such an enactment, in part because she came across as a much younger child, one in need of a great deal of assistance given the adolescent tasks at hand.

The therapy hours were now filled with talk about her struggles with the preparations for college applications, her relationship with her boyfriend, her insecurity about her looks, her lack of motivations for schoolwork, and her life at home. Clearly she was no longer waiting for me to tell her how to begin the sessions, and at times she even came wanting to figure something out, having adopted what had been my curiosity [Identification], which seemed to mark a further deepening of the treatment alliance. She was frustrated by her lack of motivation given her wish to do the work at school, or more accurately by her difficulty being alone to do the work. She increasingly recognized how insecure she feels, wanting a steady stream of assurance from others that she is special, intelligent, that they like her, and that they find her attractive. Most of all she wanted such reassurances from her boyfriend. She spoke of the lack of trust between them. I said, "it must be hard to trust that someone really wants you when you feel so undesirable yourself." She said she had not thought of this as the source of her mistrust but it made sense to her [Insight].

School continued to be a problem, and it became apparent that she would have to go to summer school to replace some low grades with higher ones. She claimed not to care about summer school. I reminded her that she tends to be out of touch with her feelings, and suggested this might be such an instance. She thought it possible although she really didn't feel bothered (not surprisingly, by the end of the summer we were both to discover that in fact she was bothered by having to spend part of the summer in school). At home, the more she recognized she had difficulties being alone, and the more she recognized this was like her mother, the more she felt some sympathy for her mother [Working Through]. She began to defend her mother against her younger sister and her father, whom she felt were on the same side against her and her mom. I pointed out that she had told me her sister cultivates a relationship with her father, whereas she has little to do with him. She admitted that she generally takes her mother's side and feels disconnected from her father, much like she sees her mother's relationship with her father. In my own mind, I began to wonder how much she was responsible for the lack of a relationship with her father.

As the summer approached she wondered if we could go to one session per week until school resumed. I pointed out my belief that it was important we continue to work intensively given that time was short given her wishes to prepare for college, her lack of motivation for school work, and her difficulties being alone. She agreed without any protest. While I thought of her response as typically compliant, I also wondered if her question about coming less often was a test—a test to see how much I wanted to see her, how much I cared about her, given her father's relative lack of involvement in her life. There did not seem to be any evidence of her being angry with me, direct or indirect, following her agreement to keep coming three times a week.

In the next sessions, she continued to report instances where she was taken advantage of, though she saw it more and more as *allowing* herself to be taken advantage of [Insight]. For example, she had a very high cell phone bill, but it was largely because her friends asked her to use it and she couldn't limit them. She did well in summer school, and it became apparent that the key factor was the amount of support she got there, like the fact that all the work was done during school hours. In other words, she did not have to do homework alone. She recognized she'd been having problems with doing the homework alone all along. Around this time, she decided to take the SAT prep course and worked the details out with her mother. Also, she came to realize early in the summer that she hated her job. Nonetheless, it took her almost the entire summer to work up the courage to give her boss two weeks' notice. When she saw that he did not have the very negative reaction she feared, she was frustrated that she hadn't left the job sooner [Working Through]. In our sessions, more and more there was an atmosphere of what she referred to as "thinking through her problems." At one point, she plainly stated that she had never used her mind to figure things out, and she was beginning to see the advantages of doing so.

At the same time, and I think not coincidentally, around the middle of the summer she began reporting some dreams. In the first dream she said, *"I was in a car in traffic with my mother. We were arguing and I hit her. A woman came from the car in front and told my mother she did not need to put up with that kind of abuse. My mother reacted by leaving . . . but then she came back and I was angry with her for leaving me. Then I drove off and left her."* She associated to a movie she'd seen recently involving parents who abandoned an unwanted child, and with a psychiatrist who tried to help the child. She thought it was a powerful dream and it made her think of how much she fears people won't like her and will leave her—the reason why she is so agreeable with most people. In thinking about how she does get angry with her mother, she recognized that she must feel more secure with her mother than just about anyone else. Also, she said she cried during the movie and that she had some of the same feelings in telling me about it [Catharsis]. I was moved by this first dream she shared with me, and in my mind it marked a further deepening of our work together, an increase in her capacity to think about her own mind rather than depending so much on me for such curiosity [Identification].

Where her boyfriend was concerned, she also was very angry and uncertain about the future of the relationship. At the same time, however, she felt very dependent on him and couldn't imagine being alone, which made her think of being away on her own at college. She wanted to continue the evenings hanging out with her boyfriend, because they made her feel everything was OK. I asked her if getting directly angry with her boyfriend was new, and she agreed it seemed different to confront him [Working Through]. In my own mind I wondered what had brought about this change. Was her awareness of her inhibitions bringing her feelings closer to the surface? Did this have something to do with her wanting to please me?

To this point, little had been said about sex, and I found myself hesitant to bring up the subject for fear of making her uncomfortable. I also identified my own sensitivities about being a male analyst with a teenage girl patient. Interestingly, her first mention of sex was about a brief kiss with a boy who was an acquaintance of her boyfriend's. She felt the kiss was a betrayal of her boyfriend, because he'd be very upset if he knew about it. At this point I recognized my collusion with her avoidance of talking about sex, and I said, "We haven't talked much about anything sexual here, like kissing boys." She told me that it was a little uncomfortable to discuss, but more it was just not much a part of her life. She and her boyfriend kissed but that was it. She was clear in her mind that she did not want to have sex and risk becoming a teenage mother. She also talked about fearing that she could want a baby, but mostly as a way to not be alone herself, like her mother. She said she knew this was not a good reason to get pregnant.

Before our summer break, for three weeks she had a significant incident with her boyfriend that took up several of our sessions. They went to a football game and he asked her to hold a beer, at which point the stadium authorities took them both for questioning. Because he was drunk, he made the whole situation worse, he was uncooperative, and he failed to protect her as she wanted him to do. She was furious with him and told him so [Catharsis and Working Through]. She could see that making her boyfriend happy is a lot of what their relationship has been for her.

She said she'd actually thought about ending the relationship with her boyfriend over the trouble at the football game. She wondered who she is apart from making others happy, and said it reminded her of her mother. Now she wanted someone to take care of her instead. She went on to describe the realization that she'd been upset her old school friends don't call her anymore, thinking they don't care, when in fact she now sees it's she who really doesn't want to hang out with them anymore [Insight]. I realized all this was coming up just before my vacation, so I said, "I wonder if you might be reacting to the fact that one of the people who does take care of you—me—will be gone for the next three weeks." She said she wasn't sure, but then she often doesn't know how she really feels. She did think it would be different not to be coming to see me for three weeks.

She was on time when we resumed after my vacation, and she filled the hour with no hesitation. She'd finally told her employer that she was leaving her job, and she even refused to stay longer when they asked if she could [Working Through]. She also told me she'd gotten into yet another fight with her younger sister, but this time she hit her sister hard in the face, scared her, and made it clear that she would no longer put up with any intimidation [Working Through]. She even said she felt some pleasure at seeing her sister afraid of her for a change. She described having a dream after this incident that was about scaring her sister and her friends. In the dream she was showing them how powerful she could be. She said it felt good to get out more of her anger, but she was surprised at how much anger there seemed to be inside of her.

Soon after this session, there was an instance where she got very angry with her father on the phone for not helping her with the college applications. She yelled at him, which was unusual, saying that he never has cared about her [Catharsis]. As it turned out, she had failed to understand that her father was quite ill. When Mary found out what had really happened, she felt a great deal of guilt and distress. When she saw him, he told her he did care about her. While he did not make eye contact with her, she said he cried. For her, this not only made her more worried about the anger in her, the way she yelled at him, but her reaction also made her realize she must care about him, to feel so guilty. This was the first time she'd considered that she might really care about him [Insight]. Interestingly, in the next session, she complained about *both* of her parents letting her younger sister get away with taking the car all the time. For the first time I could recall, she talked about both of her parents like they were a team. While I wasn't sure what it meant, I sensed a change from talking about her father as a shadow-like figure to describing him as a real person.

The remaining sessions, in the last month of this first year of the psychotherapy, focused more on her boyfriend. She was worried that college would mean leaving him behind. As she vacillated between wanting the security of her current life and wanting to move on by going to college, I sensed real confusion in her words for the first time. I asked her about this and she agreed. She described feeling more and more confused about who she is and what she wants. She was increasingly attentive to what others tell her now, because she knows that she is so inclined to please them. For the first time, she said that she wants to know what she really wants . . . for herself. In commenting on this, I said, "to go from thinking you know herself, when you really don't, to being confused, seems like an important step toward really knowing how you feel and what you want [Insight]." In the next and final second year of her treatment, before she did go on to college, the work shifted to her discovery of her own preferences, abilities, and wishes. At that point, her adolescent development seemed to be back on track.

An overview of the treatment process and the utilization of all modes of therapeutic action in this patient's treatment first reveals a process with more emphasis on direct support and introjection; in other words, a process where the therapist was more actively giving advice and that advice was establishing a presence in the patient's mind. This was necessary to stabilize the patient's deteriorating relationship with her mother and to address the dangerous academic decline. As the treatment progressed, and the more destructive symptoms decreased, the therapeutic process shifted to one where the predominant modes were insight and working through, along with some catharsis and more identification. These modes were essential to addressing the sources of the patient's low self-esteem, her anger, and her general depressive outlook on life. The point here is to appreciate that the preference for one mode of therapeutic action over another is not static over the course of a treatment, but a dynamic process that has to be monitored as the treatment progresses. By comparison, when therapists are trained to provide manualized treatments, especially ones that are highly formulaic, it is unlikely that the therapeutic process will adapt to each patient according to their individuality; instead, the patient will be expected to conform to the treatment. While it may bring about some symptomatic improvement for the patient to internalize and conform to the treatment model, as is certainly the case with some manualized treatment approaches, it will not help them find their own identity, their own voice (similar to the way that musicians speak of discovering their own unique voice with an instrument). This is not to disparage such treatments, as depending on the goals of the treatment, this may not be viewed as a problem; relief from a symptom may be all that is expected.

In the next chapter, in order to further demonstrate the centrality of these six modes of therapeutic action to all talking cures, even ones not aimed at the treatment of individuals, I take up the treatment of couples. First, it is necessary to explicate an overall conceptualization of how psychoanalytic thinking can inform the assumptions and challenges in treating couples, after which it will be possible to show the ways in which the basic modes of therapeutic action take their place in the treatment process of couples.

FIVE

The Treatment of Couples

A comprehensive computer search of all of Freud's extensive writings reveals that he used the word "unconscious" 40,162 times; by comparison, he only used the word "couples" seventeen times, there are only twenty-three times he used the word "marital," and only 168 times he used the word "marriage." Not surprisingly, however, none of these times he refers to couples, marital, or marriage is he writing about the treatment of couples. Instead, these references appear in the context of his discussing individuals, as he simply was not focused on the treatment of couples. Nonetheless, the six basic modes of therapeutic action derived from his work, being relevant to all talking cures, do inform the conceptualization of a model for treating couples and the choice of which therapeutic actions are emphasized during a particular treatment.

While Freud did not focus on treating couples, some analytic thinkers who followed him did, albeit they represent a small minority of the writers in the field. I do not intend to give a comprehensive review of all the contributions, and I will of necessity be conveying the gist of various authors' ideas. My apologies to those I have omitted, but some overview will at least convey a historical sense of post-Freudian, analytic, and even a non-analytic perspective on the treatment of couples. Dicks (1967), for example, emphasized marital tensions as arising from remaining and unmet needs (object-relational needs) from the individuals' primary relationships during childhood. Miller (1967) pointed to the fact that there are neurotic, relational patterns in dysfunctional marriages that are better revealed by treating the couple than each person individually, with an eye to pointing out the couple's tendency to externalize the blame for each one's neurotic suffering. Segraves (1978) proposed a cognitive-behavioral model for treating couples, integrating contributions from psychoanalysis, systems theory, and behaviorism. Similar to Miller,

65

though using different terms, he viewed the therapeutic action as helping each individual see the faulty schemas that are distorting their perceptions of each other. Brody (1988) stressed the need to expand a systems approach to include the interpretation of in-vivo manifestations (during the couple's sessions) of the individual psychodynamics that are repeated in the interpersonal system of the relationship. Kernberg (1991) described the importance of understanding the interaction of love and aggression, especially as they are driven by unconscious enactments of past childhood relationships in the present. His approach also included an examination of the couple's relationship as it is impacted by their differences in male and female development. Lucente (1994) devised a model of marital therapy based on an assessment of each individual according to Anna Freud's developmental lines, including object relations, moral development, psychosexuality, etc., in order to help them understand their capacities and limitations for intimacy and mature love. Sharpe (2000) used object-relational, analytic perspectives to identify seven central patterns of intimate relating, organized around two central aspects of development—connectedness and separateness. Harwood (2004) made the case that the therapist working with an individual should not follow a rigid rule against working in different modalities with the same patient; she proposed that in some cases the deep understanding gained by working with the individual patient can facilitate couples work with the same patient and their partner. Livingston (2007) wrote about the ways in which the self-psychological and intersubjective theories can inform the therapist's capacity to maintain an empathic focus capable of building the psychic structure of the couple and their capacities for emotional regulation. Shimmerlik (2008), drawing upon developments in psychoanalysis, family systems theory, the cognitive neurosciences, and infant research, looked at how couples' problems stem from their engaging in unconscious, implicit communications that foster regressive enactments. Waska (2008) wrote two papers in which he emphasized Kleinian concepts like projective identification and the concept of container-contained to understand the dynamics of a couple's relationship. In his model, there are initial meetings with each individual for assessment and establishing an alliance prior to beginning sessions as a couple. Eckardt (2010) based her ideas about couples' therapy on an integration of psychodynamic and systems perspectives, emphasizing how both individuals who make up the couple are embedded in the family and the current environment. Siegel (2012) pointed out how couples that exhibit significant denial and dissociation are often fending off the overwhelming affect associated with having been traumatized.

So here we have an overview of some of the thinking, mostly psychodynamic, about understanding and treating couples (and for the remainder of this chapter if I refer to marriage or couples I mean to include all lifetime partnerships like marriage, even if they are not formalized legally). While certainly not exhaustive, these points do represent a period ranging over forty-five years from 1967 to 2012. In some cases the emphasis is on the externalization of internal conflicts, in some the need for a systems approach, in yet others the repetition of individual psychopathology and early, disappointing object relations, while still others highlight a specific aspect of technique and therapeutic action. Some authors underscore the need for a developmental view, or the importance of empathic listening. In other words, there are numerous ideas about how to approach the treatment of couples, and as with the treatment of individuals, the essential modes of therapeutic action are not presented in a way that makes for ready comparisons between these various theories and techniques. Moreover, there is a repeated tendency to take a one-size-fit-all approach to treatment.

In order to develop a model for the assessment and the therapeutic treatment of couples that draws from all six basic modes of therapeutic action, it is important first to consider some psychoanalytic assumptions about the functioning of our individual minds and the human condition, then to examine the typical challenges in moving from infatuation to mature love, the bases for making a decision to be life partners, and finally to appreciate and assess the quality of each of the numerous partnerships that comprise lifetime relationships like marriage.

According to the latest census figures at The Center for Disease Control in Atlanta, Georgia, the divorce rate in the United States is slightly over 50 percent of the rate of marriages. Specifically, the current marriage rate is 6.8 per 1,000; the divorce rate is 3.6 per 1,000 (www.cdc.gov/nchs/fastats/divorce.htm). This statistic is not so surprising if you keep in mind that such lifetime partnerships are far more complex than other kinds of partnerships, like in business for example. Even when both individuals are reasonably stable emotionally, the complex realities, as well as the practical and emotional demands of marriage, exceed other relationships. What follows outlines some realities about the human need for relationships, as well as some basic concepts about the functioning of the human mind. Knowledge of these basic features of being human is essential: one, to appreciating the formidable challenges of marriage, of being lifetime partners; two, to understanding how to evaluate each couple's specific strengths and weaknesses; and three, to determining which modes of therapeutic action should be emphasized for a particular couple.

RELEVANT ASSUMPTIONS ABOUT BEING HUMAN

Attachment

Where relationships are concerned, a central reality about being human is that we are by our nature relational. But what does this mean?

First, and foremost its meaning is captured by Winnicott's adage (1960), "There is no such thing as a baby." This short saying captures the reality that a baby is not a viable organism and that the development of a baby cannot be understood apart from the mother-child attachment. In other words, from our earliest years our very existence depends on our attachments. Anna Freud (Midgley, 2007) observed infants and small children in the Hampstead War Nurseries, where there were long separations from parents, and extended the concept of attachment and object relations to a developmental line, with stages in the evolution of the attachment between children and parents. In fact, there are many prominent authors who have studied, theorized, observed, and documented the processes that humans go through from total dependency to being capable of independent functioning.

However, the capacity to be alone and function independently does not mean acquiring the ability to live in total isolation of others. Being a hermit is relatively rare; it's not considered normal development because our emotional need for relationships endure throughout the life cycle (Levinson, 1978; Colarusso and Nemiroff, 1981). It is this need for attachments that makes social deprivation such a powerful form of punishment and even torture.

An important consideration regarding human attachments is to appreciate that hate is not the opposite of love, as both loving and hating involve attachments. The kind of preoccupation that can be observed when there is ongoing hatred clearly betrays a strong attachment to the object of hatred. It is indifference that is the opposite of love and hate. It is indifference that represents the absence of an attachment, not really caring one way or the other.

Assumption 1: From birth to death, most humans have a powerful need for attachments. For this reason, it is important to appreciate that social conventions like marriage are the expression of a fundamental human need. It is also important to appreciate love is not the opposite of hate, in that they are both forms of attachment, whereas indifference is the opposite of love and hate.

The Mind in Conflict

Following on Freud's work and a number of psychoanalysts who followed him, Brenner (1982) wrote directly that mental conflict is not an occurrence at the point of some mental disorder, but that it is always present, both waking and sleeping. For this reason, he chose to title the book, *The Mind in Conflict*. Thus, mental life is to be understood as a series of compromises between desires, aggression, ideals, inner prohibitions, emotions, cognitive abilities, and external reality; all of which interact under normal conditions to maximize pleasure, to minimize pain, and to anticipate and protect us from dangers. To further complicate matters, dangers in the mind can be real, imagined, or both. What is more, the ability to distinguish between real and imagined dangers is a function of the conscious mind. In the unconscious mind, distinctions between reality and fantasy are not maintained. Just think of the fantastical nature of dreams, mental phenomena that take place when the mind is not functioning consciously. All of us must deal with the fact that external realities demand some pleasures be denied, deferred, or satisfied indirectly.

Assumption 2: Where there does not appear to be any conflict in an individual's mind, it means that the conflicts are being managed successfully, not that they are absent. Thus, at the interface of two individuals that make up a couple, there are two minds in continuous conflict, much of which will be unconscious.

The Complex Role of Emotions

All emotions function as signals, as information. Anxiety, for example, is a signal of danger, which can be real, imagined, or both. Our emotions not only function as signals that provide information to us as we experience them, the outward expression of our emotions is a signal to others. Anger often signals a reaction to distress, aggression released by distress: real, imagined, or both. But anger is often a second emotion, after feeling hurt, for example. The anger can occur so quickly as the second emotion, that it is possible for the first emotion to not consciously register in the person's mind. Emotions are plastic such that they can be displaced, reversed, suppressed, somatized, externalized and projected, rationalized, etc. For these reasons, the effectiveness of the signal function of our emotions can be subverted, even creating confusion and misunderstanding.

When emotions reach sufficient intensity that they interfere with the ability to think, they become traumatic, not informative. There are two forms this emotional trauma can take. In acute emotional trauma something occurs that is so distressing it is overwhelming. One example would be the death of a child. By comparison, there is a much more insidious form of trauma called cumulative trauma, which refers to distress that can be tolerated with limited exposure, but that occurs so many times it eventually becomes overwhelming. An example might be someone poking you once in the arm, which is not very distressing, as compared to someone poking you in the same place, hundreds of time, such that over time the spot become increasingly sensitive and painful, to a point that is traumatic.

Assumption 3: Our emotions function as signals to others, and ourselves; as such they are an essential component of a couple's ability to communicate effectively. When emotions undergo transformations that sabotage their ability to function as effective signals, couples will have difficulties with communications. For example, when hurt is expressed as anger, it is more likely to evoke defensiveness in a partner than sympathy.

Sometimes, couples fail to cope with an acute emotional trauma, leading to problems in their relationship. More often, however, couples get into difficulties because of cumulative traumas, where the repetition of separately tolerable, emotionally distressing interactions has led to those moments being overwhelming, leading to a quantity of emotional distress that interferes with the capacity for rational thought.

Individual Personality Structure

Melanie Klein was one of the first contributors to introduce developmental ideas about object relations into Freudian thinking. She used the word "position" to label what she was to describe as the two basic stages of development from an early, narcissistic level personality structure, that she called the paranoid-schizoid position (Klein, 1946), to what, under favorable conditions of childhood development, becomes a more mature capacity for relating to others, that she called the depressive position (Klein, 1952). While there are many aspects of Klein's ideas that remain developmentally questionable, both in terms of her attribution of psychological capacities to very young infants, and in terms of her theoretical speculations, the two positions she described do differentiate what I will refer to as immature object relations from mature object relations. These positions refer to more stable aspects of an individual's personality, and as such are an important aspect of assessing each person's personality structure, as it will impact the capacity to relate. While there is a continuum from immature to mature object relations, the qualities of each will become apparent as the therapist sees the couple relating.

Immature Object Relations: People who have not developed beyond the position of emotionally immature object relations will possess several qualities of relating that are important to assess. First, they will have difficulty holding positive and negative feelings for someone at the same time. Instead, they will be prone to idealize and devalue, to divide their experiences into good and bad, and rather than maintain mixed feelings, their experience with others and themselves will be highly dependent on how they feel at any given moment. As a result, rather than having a unified experience of the people in their life and of themselves, they will tend to have un-integrated relationships and a diffuse sense of their own identities, leading to patterns of confusion and chaos in their interactions with others. If this were not problem enough, those with immature object relations will be prone to unconsciously transfer their bad feelings into others, being unable to contain and tolerate the feelings, and then they will be inclined to relate to others according to those negative distortions, often provoking others into identifying with and acting out these negative feelings.

The greatest challenge to couples, however, is that immature object relations interfere with the ability to experience others as separate people, with their own feelings, thoughts, wishes, desires, and frustrations. This means that the capacity for empathy is at best very limited. Others are experienced as need gratifiers or as frustrating, or as alternating between the two, but not as a whole person with all those qualities. For couples, if one or the other is struggling with immature object relations they will not have the ability to embrace the fact that a healthy relationship has to make the space for two subjective realities. Another result is an inability to get beyond struggles over who is right and who is wrong, to a mature interaction in which the couple strives to understand each other, even when their perspectives are quite different.

Mature Object Relations: People who have developed emotionally to the capacity for mature object relations can simultaneously hold both positive and negative feelings toward others and themselves, making it possible to sustain an integrated experience of both. As a result, how the person feels at a given moment does not determine the perceptions of what is going on in relationships. As a result, there is far less interpersonal distortion and less interpersonal coercion, and, instead there is a sense of continuity in both the relationship and the individual's experience of their own identity. Most important, these emotionally mature capacities mean the couple can create a space in their relationship that can embrace their different experiences and perceptions; this space is essential for a couple to have empathy for each other.

Assumption 4: Our relationships will be significantly impacted by the extent to which our partners and we have or have not developed the capacity for mature object relations. These positions, determined by our development from childhood, shape who we are and how we cope. These positions are embedded in our personality structures on a formal level, and as such tend not to be conscious, meaning that couples are not likely to identify this potential source of their difficulties or to even put it into words. Individuals with severe forms of immature object relations present a significant challenge to couples treatment; in such cases, a couple's treatment outcome often depends on intensive, concurrent individual psychotherapy.

Implications for Being a Couple: First, humans have a basic drive for attachments and to be in relationships, so the motivation to find life partners is the expression of a very fundamental human need. Being alone like a hermit is not in our nature. Second, each of our minds is always in conflict; what appears to be the absence of conflict is in fact the product of successful compromises between the conflicts in our minds. Thus, conflicts between couples are likely given the ever-present challenges of working out the conflicts in our individual minds. Third, an understanding of the functioning of our emotions is essential to assessing a couple's strengths and weaknesses. The capacity to use one's own feelings as information and to appreciate others' emotions as providing information is essential to successful communications. Furthermore, it is critical to understand the potential for emotional trauma that is not acute but cumulative. Couples often fail to appreciate the impact of cumulative trauma, as it has developed due to an insidious repetition of years of painful interactions, each of which on its own does not appear traumatic. And fourth, it is important to evaluate the developmental level of object relations in each partner, as each partner's personality structure will have a great impact on the couple's potential for empathy, especially their capacity to create a space between them for two subjective realities, rather than one or both of them insisting that their point of view is the right one.

DEFINING LOVE

In order to assess a couple's relationship it is necessary to pursue an understanding of their definition of love and of the degree of maturation between them. Frequently, the word "love" is used without any clear understanding of how it is being used. Saying "I love you" can hold very different meanings. Does it refer to a good feeling in the one who is expressing love? Does it refer to admiration for the beloved? Or, does it refer to a commitment between the couple, to each other? In fact, it can refer to all these things at different stages in the progression of a couple's relationship.

Infatuation: At first, the experience of what is often called love, in the early stages of a couple's relationship, is often better described as infatuation—a feeling based on having so little knowledge of the other person that beyond their physical appearance, they are more a narcissistic fantasy than a reality. The less you know about someone the freer you are to experience him or her as the embodiment of your own wishes. They are a container for all the desired qualities. Such relationships are not grounded in reality but based more on fantasy. This kind of love is in essence narcissistic and more about the lover than the beloved.

Nonetheless, such relationships are intense, compelling, and intoxicating, albeit unsustainable. Why? Because as you get to know the person better, his or her real qualities inevitably do not fulfill all the imagined ones. Thus, the state of mind sometimes referred to as being "love sick" gives way to reality, which may be perceived as falling out of love, in which case the relationship loses the dynamic that held it together. For this reason, it is generally not a good idea to make important decisions like marriage during this infatuation phase of a relationship. By comparison, the appeal of affairs is that they often provide a more sustainable state of infatuation, given that the extent of involvement is usually limited and the relationship can remain based more on fantasy.

Mature Adult Love: Perhaps there is no more elegant description of mature adult love than in Shakespeare's sonnet 116 (Burrow, 2002). In this sonnet about love he says, "Love is not love which alters . . . when it alteration finds." Throughout the sonnet he repeatedly makes the point that mature love is not threatened by disagreements or conflicts, by life's challenges, by changes in the loved one, including the changes that come with age and time. In other words, he defines love as a commitment, not a feeling, and since love is not based on feeling good, those times when a couple's relationship feels distressing does not mean that love is lost. Love is the commitment. From this point of view, the opposite of hatred might be called affection, not love.

So to establish mature love, the couple must be able to move from fantasies of each other to an acceptance of their realities. They have to trust in one another, with honesty, even when it might be painful. There has to be recognition of the difference between privacy and secrecy, so there is not an expectation of knowing each other's every thought and feeling; secrecy is reserved for areas of mutual agreement, like having an affair if there has been a promise of monogamy. The couple has to embrace the capacity for real forgiveness, where it is possible to move on without lingering feelings of surrender or resentment. With aging, there has to be a mutual acceptance of changing appearance, abilities, and sexuality. One indication of mature adult love will be the experience that times apart create a greater appreciation for one another.

THE CHALLENGE OF MULTIPLE PARTNERSHIPS

In considering the challenges of marriage and other forms of life partnerships, and looking at the striking failure rate of these couples' relationships, it is crucial to recognize that there are many, many partnerships included in such relationships. To name some of the more salient ones, they include partners to have a sexual relationship; partners to be friends and confidants; partners in relating to each other's friends and families; partners to maintain a home; partners to manage finances; partners (often) to be parents and raise children; as well as being partners to plan for aging and taking care of each other. While this is not an exhaustive list, consider the challenges of having one relationship bear all these different partnerships. As a relationship moves from infatuation to mature love, the couple has to assess their compatibilities, areas of incompatibility, and whether or not any of the incompatibilities are deal breakers, like a basic disagreement on the desire to have or not have children. While all couples will have some areas of compatibility and incompatibility, clearly the more the balance favors compatibilities the better the prognosis for their future together, but the capacity to be flexible over time is equally as important given that the years can influence the balance between being compatible and incompatible.

ASSESSMENT

All the factors mentioned to this point are important to assess the strengths and challenges for a given couple. What is the nature of their attachment? What is the status of each of their minds in terms of coping with conflict? Do either one or both need to be in their own individual treatment? In terms of Melanie Klein's positions, to what extent is each of them capable of mature object relations? What is each one's capacity for mature love? How does each of them experience, or not experience, their emotions: how do they communicate, or not communicate, their feelings to each other? Is there evidence of either acute or cumulative trauma?

Next, it is important to go over all the different partnerships they have as a couple and assess the functionality or dysfunctionality of each partnership. From one couple to another there can be very different problem areas in terms of which partnerships are succeeding and which are not. It is also important to evaluate how each of them defines love: do they define love as a feeling or as a commitment? Thus, these areas of evaluation cover the extent of their compatibility, the nature of their commitment to each other, their capacity for compassion for each other, the quality of their communications with each other, their ability to cooperate with each other, and lastly their ability to compromise with each other. In these areas I have found all couples differ, making it impossible to have a formulaic, manualized approach to the treatment of couples.

RECOMMENDATIONS AND TREATMENT

Hopefully, it is clear by now that the very process of assessment of the couple cannot be separated from the treatment itself. Why? Because they are learning a great deal about themselves in terms of their strengths, their challenges, and their views of being a couple, as they go through the assessment process. Thus, by the time the therapist is ready to make recommendations, a great deal of education has taken place [Direct Support] and the couple knows themselves better [Insight]. Often, in the course of the evaluation emotions will be expressed as well. When this takes the form of defensive aggression it tends to be destructive, and by mutual agreement it should not be allowed once identified as such, but when it is the expression of hurt [Catharsis], there can be increased compassion for each other.

There are some general psychoanalytic principles and an attitude that will apply to all couples' treatments. First is appreciating that it is not the therapist's right or responsibility to take a moral stand on what the couple decides will be the fate of their relationship. This should be stated from the outset, including the possibility that if the couple decides not to be together the therapist will remain available to assist in that process. The therapist is not there to impose views about how life should be lived, nor what marriage should be or how it should be done. There is no model of a "perfect couple." Instead, the emphasis is realistic and on the idea of a "good enough marriage."

The overall aim is to assist in identifying dysfunctional patterns, conscious and unconscious, in order to promote awareness and the capacity to make more functional, adaptive choices. In other words, to help the couple make the most informed decisions possible. There is an assumption that life is ambivalent. Most realities involve mixed feelings, and the challenge is to reconcile ambivalent feelings in a way that maximizes pleasure and adaptation, and minimizes suffering. The assessment will include gathering the information described above and confronting the couple for more information, especially where it seems important information is missing. This process will also include the need to clarify any areas that seem incomplete, confusing, or contradictory, and the interpretation of any maladaptive patterns according to the unconscious motives that maintain those patterns. Recommendations for couple's treatment, and possibly for the individual treatment of one or both partners will clarify all these discoveries.

As with all analytic treatments, it will be important to establish an atmosphere of discovery and rationality, without any promises of a specific outcome. It will be critical that both partners share the goals of the treatment. Assisting the couple to accept the findings can be one of the greater challenges of the treatment and can take time. Emphasizing the strengths in the partnership will be a critical balance to the pain of looking at its failures. And finally, there will be an ongoing effort to help the couple see where they are reacting to what they imagine about each other rather than what is real.

But first, it will be helpful to review the generic modes of therapeutic action in working with couples. First there is Direct Support, which includes the education about being a couple, advice, emotional support and empathy, and at times directly intervening when the couple is engaging in dysfunctional patterns of communication (it is important to let the couple know you will do this at the beginning of treatment and to get their permission to interrupt them). Second, Catharsis will be an important part of the treatment, where the therapist is facilitating the experience and expression of emotion, demonstrating the constructive expression of aggression as healthy assertiveness, the power of expressing hurt when it's been masked by anger, and the binding impact of expressing loving feelings. Third, the therapist can serve as a role model, sometimes by self-disclosure, which will promote both Introjection and Identification; I will refer to this below as Modeling. And fourth, Insight will help the couple to understand their emotions, to see things in a new way, and to recognize the motives behind dysfunctional patterns of relating in order to find adaptive ones. Helping them see that anger is frequently not the first emotion, even though it's the first one they are consciously aware of having. Insight also includes the recognition of the many reasons that life partnerships and marriage are inherently challenging for most people, so they can identify the multiple partnerships that each require attention. Lastly, couples need to repeat new patterns before the old ones will reliably change, so there is the critical need for Working Through. Beyond these general principles of technique, however, it is not possible to be prescriptive and generalize about the individualized treatments of all couples, so what follows are eight brief summaries of different treatment scenarios that the couple's therapist can encounter, with reference to the modes of therapeutic action more effective for each scenario. These are examples but by no means exhaustive of all the scenarios encountered with different couples, which would be impossible.

SPECIFIC EXAMPLES OF COUPLES TREATMENT

1. "Our problem turned out to be we're such nice people, we're both so uncomfortable with aggression that we are not setting limits on our children and they are running our lives. Our therapist helped us to understand our child's need for limits, he talked about his own children, and he helped us to see our frustration as more normal [Direct Support, Modeling, and Insight]. Now that we see what is healthy aggression, we're setting limits, our child is sleeping, and we have time for ourselves again. It was not easy at first but over time we came to see it was more functional." [Working Through]

2. "We both suffered so much damage as children, we are so prone to feel that we have been treated unfairly, and we are both so vulnerable to feeling an intolerable sense of shame, that we react to conflict by defensive anger and needing to blame each other . . . we can't get past this, we've both been in our own therapy for years, we've really tried. We just can't be together." [Insight]

3. "We never realized that we needed to consider that our marital partnership has to be coordinated like any business does . . . so we need to have regular meetings. You told us about how you and your wife need to have a meeting every Sunday morning to discuss the week. Now that we're meeting like that our lives are working much better." [Direct Support, Modeling, Insight]

4. "I've been vulnerable to depression all my life, and I'm just able to admit it and how it has inhibited my sexual drive. I can be more assertive in connecting to my spouse but it's hard when I'm depressed. My spouse has a neurotic need to be in control and prefers masturbation to the possibility of rejection by me, which only increases my depression. As we both appreciate this pattern, we have been able to begin to make new efforts at connecting and talking about our feelings." [Direct Support, Insight, Working Through]

5. "We cannot get along because I don't feel the same about you as I did when we met. It was magical at first, and now I feel disappointed in you. It has helped me to begin to express some of my disappointment, but I don't know if I can tolerate the disillusionment. Maybe I can see that my expectations are unrealistic, and if I find someone else this will happen all over again, but it's very difficult. My mother told me good boys get everything they want when they grow up. Clearly that is not true but more how she got me to comply with her wishes. I feel angry with her but understand she was not able to tolerate much frustration herself. I am just going to have to keep working at this for it to change." [Direct Support, Insight, Catharsis, Working Through]

6. "We now see that we have different priorities in our life goals. You want to emphasize security (saving money) and I want us to live in as much affluence as possible (spending money). We've been unable to communicate, because we've not respected each other's priorities. Neither one of us will tolerate feeling invalidated. It helped us that you shared with us some of how you and your wife can have these difficulties. Now seeing that respecting each other's preferences does not mean losing all control, maybe we can work out a compromise. It will take time." [Direct Support, Insight, Modeling, Working Through]

7. "We didn't realize that we are both so busy, with so many responsibilities, that neither of us has any emotional reserve. Any stressor causes us to fight with each other, as we don't feel safe to direct it at our children, our boss, or friends. As hard as it is to do, we need to set some priorities and offload some of our commitments. If we don't . . . we will continue to dump the stress into our partnership. We just cannot ask that much of our relationship. We are beginning to make changes but it is hard, and we have to stay with it." [Direct Support, Insight, Working Through]

8. "I now see that when I get angry . . . all my thoughts go to everything negative . . . only making me more and more angry, until I
   explode. Then when I provoke you enough, you get angry back
   and I feel justified in my anger. I do need you to be patient with me
   since this is not going to be easy to change, but I appreciate your
   love (commitment) and want you to know how important you are
   to me. I haven't been doing this intentionally, but now that I see it I
   have to take responsibility for it, which means getting into my own
   treatment." [Direct Support, Insight]

CONCLUSIONS: As with the previous chapter, which covered the details of an individual treatment, and the role of the six generic modes of
therapeutic action, this chapter on the treatment of couples demonstrates
the reliance on those same therapeutic actions, but in a very different
type of psychotherapy. Couples need to be educated about the challenges
of being a couple, about the functioning of their own minds, and the
interface between the two. While the therapist relies on these basic modes
of therapeutic action, whether or not they are explained to the couple
depends on the particular treatment. At times modeling to promote introjection and identification is best accomplished without any explanation of
the reasons for modeling, whereas it can be critical that the couple under-
stands the behavioral principles associated with working through so they
understand the reason why change can be hard and slow.

In the next chapter, I make a significant shift from discussing the basic
modes of therapeutic action in the treatment of couples to talking about
different psychoanalysts' theories of how psychoanalysis effects change.
Despite the dramatic difference in these two modalities of treatment, it
will be possible to see how the same basic modes of therapeutic action are
involved in the process of how talking cures.

SIX

Deconstructing Psychoanalytical Concepts of Cure

What follows is an analysis of a sample of various views of the psychoanalytic treatment process, mostly more recent, from a PEP-WEB search of psychoanalytic articles that specifically refer to "therapeutic action" in the title (PEP refers to the *Psychoanalytic Electronic Publishing* website, a searchable database of psychoanalytic literature). The authors' views are first described and then analyzed according to their relative emphasis or deemphasis of the six basic modes of therapeutic action outlined above. This not only demonstrates a method for deconstructing contrasting opinions about the analytic process, it also permits a more comparative assessment of them.

Others have noted the need for a way to deconstruct different views of why talking cures in psychoanalysis. Michels (2007), for example, after reviewing a number of authors who contributed their views of therapeutic action in a volume devoted to it, speaks directly to this need. First, Michels summarizes various authors' views, and then he concludes, "We have a lively and enthusiastic dialogue about therapeutic action in psychoanalysis. The participants in this collection articulate their views and develop them forcefully. A major problem for the field of psychoanalysis is that we have not yet developed a strategy or a language for comparing, testing, or evaluating these—for selecting from among them, for discarding some, or, more likely, selecting aspects of some and discarding others, developing creative combinations and evaluating the results. This is the challenge for the future." To his point, it is precisely this challenge that I take up here.

Before considering specific authors' ideas, however, it is interesting to look at the number of articles a PEP-WEB search yields for each of the important terms under examination. First, a search for the words "therapeutic action" anywhere in an article yields 3,092 references whereas "talking cure" yields 1,022 references (or hits as they are referred to in the search jargon). When you combine "therapeutic action and insight" you get 239 hits; search for "therapeutic action" in the title of articles and you get 151 hits, combine "therapeutic action and identification" and you get seventy-one hits; combine "therapeutic action and working through" and you get fifty-nine hits; combine "therapeutic action and introjection" and you get thirteen hits; combine "therapeutic action and catharsis" and you get twelve hits; lastly, combine "therapeutic action and support" and you get nine hits. Thus, in the literature there are far more articles and books that refer to "therapeutic action" and "talking cures" than to these specific modes of therapeutic action. Among the six modes of therapeutic action taken from Freud's work, the greatest number of hits is for Insight by a factor of four, then Identification, Working Through, Introjection, Catharsis, and the least hits is Direct Support. This is not surprising given that the history of psychoanalytic technique has emphasized insight over all else as the curative factor. The fact that identification comes in second is understandable given the increasing concern with the relational aspects of therapeutic action in more recent years.

Beyond such general considerations, what follows is an evaluation of the differences and similarities of specific authors' ideas about the therapeutic action(s) of psychoanalytic treatment (primarily psychoanalysis). The various views are presented chronologically in order to see if there are any identifiable trends over time. For the sake of this chapter, I have only chosen those articles that had the words "therapeutic action" in the title. Overall there were 151 hits, but when articles of book reviews and panel reports were eliminated there were fewer, and in some cases one author wrote several articles on the same theme, so I chose the one that gave the clearest definition of therapeutic action.

As a format to review the authors, and then deconstruct their views, the author's view will come first in each paragraph, followed by a breakdown of their view according to the six modes of therapeutic action. For the ease of the reader, each author's view of the analytic process is briefly described in regular font, followed by the deconstruction of their views on how talking cures in italics, with the primary modes of therapeutic action in [brackets]. Also, I want to be clear that these are my views, based on my reading of the authors, and it is quite possible some authors might not agree with my reading of what they have written or with my method of deconstruction. Nonetheless, I believe that such an effort has to begin somewhere. Please keep in mind that in some cases the authors' views are more explicit and clear than in others, so in some cases I am not as definitive as in others.

Menninger (1958) believed that analytic psychotherapy was effective only insofar as it successfully included support and emotional experience and insight. *Thus, in speaking of the analytic process of psychoanalytic psycho-therapy he emphasized [direct support], as well as [catharsis] and [insight].*

Modell (1976) focused on the idea that the analytic process provides an illusion of safety and protection that he called the "holding environment." In his view, with the transference neuroses, this holding environment is a container that allows the transference neurosis to unfold so it can be interpreted, whereas for the narcissistic neuroses, the analysis of magical fantasies associated with the holding environment facilitates ego consolidation that is needed for the transference neurosis to emerge in an analyzable form. *In other words, the holding environment can be thought of as a [direct supportive] mode of therapeutic action, brought about through the analytic process. While this is only a container in the case of the transference neuroses, making the transference neurosis available for interpretation and [insight], for the narcissistic disorders the holding environment facilitates the analysis and insight of magical fantasies associated with the holding environment itself, after which, interpretation and insight of the transference neurosis is possible. Modell believed that the failure to appreciate this two-step process in the case of the narcissistic neuroses resulted in the holding environment remaining a form of [direct support] that the patient would need in perpetuity.*

For patients with self-pathology, who require excessive praise, Kohut and Wolfe (1978) advocated an approach that emphasizes empathic listening and acceptance of the patient's narcissistic defenses against unmet emotional needs from childhood, thereby creating an atmosphere where old needs can slowly emerge as the patient becomes more self-empathic. They proposed that if the old needs are mobilized in this way, in time they will gradually and spontaneously be transformed into normal assertiveness and a normal allegiance to ideals, in part through the patient's increased self-awareness with self-acceptance. *Kohut and Wolfe seem to be describing a form of [direct support]; specifically a kind of empathic listening that minimizes shame and promotes the expression of archaic emotional needs, rather than processes of internalization like introjection or identification. In conjunction, they describe how this empathic listening leads to interpretation and [insight] about archaic emotional needs and expectations (e.g., mirror transferences), which promotes more mature narcissism and the more typical analytic process characteristic of patients who do not have self-pathology.*

Abend (1979) focused on the idea that a patient's personal theory of how analysis cures often shapes how the patient participates in the analytic process. Unconscious determinants of the patients' theories can turn out to be infantile sexual fantasies connected with their unconscious wishes for instinctual satisfaction. Similar unconscious fantasies can influence analysts' theories about how analysis works. Abend describes how the analysis of such influences may be an important factor in the therapeutic action of the treatment. *Abend considers patients' theories of cure as one important area of focus for interpretation, in order to facilitate [insight] into how they approach the analytic situation. He does interestingly suggest that*

the analyst's views of how analysis cures may also be influenced by such fanta-
sies, making it equally important that the analyst has insight about his/her own
unconscious fantasies, as they impact the analytic process.

Greenberg (1981) compared Sullivan and Fairbairn and concluded
that despite the differences in their terminologies, their essential views of
therapeutic action are basically the same. Both emphasize that change
comes about as a result of the analyst's use of him or herself as a new
person who can gain entry into the closed inner world of the patient.
Sullivan talks of the understanding by the patient of distortions of others
based on one's own fantasies, that is, of learning about the real (viz.,
"new") object, while Fairbairn emphasizes instead the substitution of
"natural objects" — those of the external world — for pathological internal
objects. *In both cases, the emphasis is on internalization, either of "a new per-*
son" or "natural objects." Whether the mechanisms are [identification] and/or
[introjection], the recognition of distortions also points to some role for [insight].

According to Blum (1981), the resolution of unconscious conflict does
not necessarily repair developmental failures. He differentiated structural conflict from structural deficit, with the belief that the analytic treatment of structural deficits will be of limited effectiveness. He also said
that "analytic change" does not require a transference cure or a cure
through the "real" relationship though did recognize non-interpretive
elements that may be therapeutically beneficial and promote development. *Thus, Blum recognizes mechanisms of therapeutic action that occur dur-*
ing psychoanalysis other than interpretation and insight, but he views these non-
interpretative elements as "therapeutically beneficial." Thus, he limits the con-
cept of "analytic change" to the therapeutic action brought about by interpreta-
tion and [insight].

While not specifically writing exclusively about the process of psychoanalysis, Rosenblatt (1987), in an article called "Change in Psychotherapy," specified several modes of therapeutic action for the process of
psychoanalytically informed psychotherapies. He felt that the most stable
changes included those resulting from insight and identification, which
often operate to stimulate and facilitate each other. At the same time, he
noted that more temporary and fragile changes are apt to result from
magical expectations in individuals who develop inconstant introjections.
In this article, Rosenblatt explicitly refers to the mechanisms of insight, identifi-
cation, and introjection. He views [insight] and [identification] as leading to
more lasting changes than [introjection], which he views as a developmentally
less mature mechanism of change.

Meissner (1989) wrote about how the moderately positive and constructive aspects of the transference make the analyst a relatively benign
and supportive object for the patient's introjection. He said this process
creates what he called the "analytic introject" (Meissner, 1979), which
replaces the more pathogenic introjects that lie at the core of the patient's
pathological sense of self and serve as the basis of his neurotic distur-

bance. As the analytic process ensues, the "analytic introject" is repro-cessed by identifications, complemented by ongoing identifications with the analyst that come from the therapeutic alliance. He felt these inter-woven processes bring about the internal change in the patient that the analytic process seeks to accomplish, where the contribution of interpre-tation is facilitative. *Thus, Meissner explicitly emphasizes [introjection] and [identification] as the modes of therapeutic action, referring to interpretation and [insight] in a manner secondary to the quality of the analytic relationship.*

Gray (1990) emphasized that therapeutic action is derived from the analyst and patient sharing observations of the patient's resistance to drive derivatives, briefly allowed into consciousness. He felt that process-es of ego maturation are set in motion by intellectually gained and experi-entially exercised insights. *Thus, Gray explicitly prioritizes the mobilization of ego maturation by the acquisition and implementation of [insights], and by [working through], which he refers to as experiential exercise.*

In Schwaber's view (1990), psychoanalysis brings about change by the patient having a new experience, fostered by the analyst's interpreta-tions, leading to a sense of discovery and expanding recognition of his or her inner world. In fact, Schwaber is quite clear in saying, "This is the mode of therapeutic action." *This is quite clear and explicitly refers to [inter-pretation] as the mode of therapeutic action.*

Stolorow (1993) emphasizes the impact of the transference meanings of psychoanalytic interpretations, but he does not discount other sources of therapeutic action, like those that may derive from non-interpretive aspects of the analytic process. One of his main points is that psychoana-lytic interpretations derive their power to effect change from the inter-subjective matrix in which they crystallize. *First, there is a clear indication of the primacy of [interpretation] as a mode of therapeutic action, and other modes are not dismissed; but there is an additional consideration here having to do with the intersubjective relationship between patient and analyst. It is more than the content of the words spoken in an interpretation, but it is this intersubjective experience as well. While the precise mechanism is not specified here, I suspect the important and regressive nature of the analytic relationship is at work, and enhancing modes of internalization, whether it be [identification] and/or [intro-jection].*

Chused (1996), in a paper on therapeutic action, said it is the disso-nance between the patient's transference expectations and the analyst's behavior that creates the opportunity for therapeutic action through dis-covering and interpreting transferences. *Thus, she emphasizes [insight] as a primary mode of therapeutic action, achieved through recognizing the discrepan-cy between the analyst as a real object and as a transference object.*

Jacobs (1990) wrote of the "corrective emotional experience," and the idea that internalization of some of the analyst's attitudes, values, ego capacities, and superego traits inevitably takes place alongside the acqui-sition of insight, contributing to the therapeutic effect of analysis. He recognized that including such internalizations as a part of the therapeutic action of psychoanalysis has often been denigrated as non-analytic because, for the most part, it operates non-interpretively and outside of conscious awareness; but he maintains that such processes of internalization continue throughout the life span and contribute to structural change. *Clearly, Jacobs accepts that there are many contributions to the therapeutic action of psychoanalysis, including [introjection] and [identification] as well as [insight].*

Loewald (1960) felt that the analyst, through the objective interpretation of transference distortions, increasingly becomes available to the patient as a new object, one who helps the patient appreciate distortions in a core sense of self and others. If the analyst is sufficiently objective and neutral, and remains true to this emerging core in the patient, the analyst will not impose a concept of what the patient should become, but rather will convey the analyst's love and respect for the patient's individuality. *Here Loewald focuses predominantly on interpretation and [insight] as the main therapeutic modality. He emphasizes that the therapeutic action should avoid mechanisms of introjection and identification that would impose on the patient the analyst's image of what the patient should become. He encourages a [depersonalized identification] with the analyst's analyzing function, with the analyst's love and respect for the individual, that leads the patient to have the independent capacity for insight, including both an observing capacity and an appreciation for how the mind works.*

Describing therapeutic action in working with children, Caspary (1993) emphasizes in describing a case that the therapeutic gains were shown to be directly related to the patient's development of the capacity to empathize with his or her own self-representations, as experienced and communicated by the therapist. *Thus, in Caspary's work with children, the therapeutic action is viewed as the result of the child's [identification] with the therapist's version of the child, as played back to the child, resulting in the child having a greater capacity for empathizing with him or herself.*

Hoffman (1994) states that therapeutic action derives from the fact that the analyst is an authority, which does not get analyzed, but is conveyed by the analyst and received and integrated by the patient. He views the analytic process, when it has been helpful, as including a factor of affirmation that comes from the analyst. *Here it would appear there is some form of internalization of the analyst by the patient. It is difficult to tell from this statement to what extent Hoffman is referring to [introjection] or [identification] or both. The fact that he says this form of therapeutic action does not get analyzed suggests he views analyzing more along conventional lines of [interpretation]. Since this article was published in 1994, still a transitional period in psychoanalysis from an orthodox model where interpretation is the sole mode of therapeutic action, it is not surprising he distinguishes the internalization of the analyst's affirmation from analyzing, whereas with all six modes of*

*therapeutic action included in the process of analyzing, such unempirical defer-
ence to previous ways of thinking is rendered less likely.*

Rustin (1997) writes that "there is therapeutic action in a psychoanalytic stance that explicitly acknowledges the intersubjective matrix, emphasizes affect and state, and advocates systematic inquiry into the impact of the analytic activity on the patient." This process both recognizes
and validates the patient's sense of agency, and empowers the patient to
shape the treatment in a way that fits, by being more active rather than
passive, thus enhancing a subjective experience of agency in the patient.
*The very idea of "inquiry" points to the presence of [insight] in the therapeutic
action, but this description seems more complex, as the patient being able to
shape the treatment suggests that the analyst is conforming to the patient's
needs, which could be viewed as a form of [direct support]. At the same time, the
changes in the patient's self-experience also suggest some [identification] with
this new experience of an object relationship.*

According to Summers (1997), who bases his theory of the analytic
process on some of the ideas of Winnicott, the main ingredient of therapeutic action is the internalization of a new object relationship, partly
created and partly given, out of the transitional space provided by the
analyst. He says that the creation of this new object relationship can be a
lengthy, "tortuous" process because it requires the abandonment of familiar experiences of self and other. *Thus, Summers says that the "crucial
ingredient of therapeutic action" is the internalization of a new object relationship, although he does not specify if he differentiates between [introjection and
identification]. He also refers to the pain of giving up previous experiences of self
and other, so it seems he views analysis as a process of grieving; the use of the
word "tortuous" suggests [catharsis] is important for this grief process.*

According to Aron (2000), "at the end of an analysis it is not insight or
other knowledge of psychic content that would best demonstrate the
patient's growth or the success of the treatment, but rather it is the capacity for self-reflexivity." *Here [insight] about content is seen as not being the
primary agent in promoting the capacity for self-reflexivity, a most desired treatment outcome. Instead, Aron thinks that this capacity is born of a "triangular
mental space" between analysts and their analysands, an intersubjective space in
which both experience new discoveries such that the process itself is internalized.
Thus, it would appear that [identification] is important here, but it is the identification of a process between and in between the patient and analyst, not with
the analyst per se.*

O'Connell (2000) describes mechanisms of therapeutic action characteristic based on dyadic versus triadic object relations. In the dyadic
mode, the analyst responds with aspects of his or her self that mirror the
patient's subjectivity, bringing the patient's experience into a place where
it can then be seen and known. By contrast, in the triadic mode, the
analyst keeps in mind the patient's need to locate his or her self in a
context, and invites the patient to see him or herself not only from inside

the patient's own space, but also from the perspective of others. *The focus on the idea of making it possible to see and know suggests an analytic process that is emphasizing [insight] while O'Connell may well include other modes of therapeutic action, the focus here is more on the developmental level of object relations as they impact the analytic process, more than on the specific mode(s) of therapeutic action; in other words, more on how to work with the patient than what brings about change.*

In another article from the one referred to before, Summers (2001) says that it is critical to provide patients with a therapeutic space that promotes the experience and realization of changes. He makes it clear that while he believes the analytic process and analytic change come in many forms including interpretation, internalization of functions, and the analyst's emotional impact on the patient, he also expressed the conviction that the patient must use the analyst's offerings to live a new experience. *Here Summers recognizes the value of [insight], [introjection], [identification], and [catharsis], but he goes on to emphasize the importance of patients realizing and experiencing change, emphasizing the importance of [working through] within the analysis itself.*

Stern (2002), in presenting a more relational and intersubjective approach to psychoanalysis, describes situations during the treatment when the patient feels newly recognized by the analyst, as opposed to the experiences based on archaic transferences. He says that these momentary identifications strengthen the patient's relationship to himself or herself and generate feelings of cohesion, vitality, and substantiality. *Here we see a view of therapeutic action that is clearly stressing [identification] as a primary mode.*

Seligman (2003), in describing the evolution of relational theory, points to there being various modes of therapeutic action that are synergistic, not exclusive. He includes insight, the interruption of archaic relational patterns, and a holding environment for the patient, as well as empathy and the working through of disturbances in the treatment relationship. He also speaks of patients having access to new interpersonal experiences with the analyst. *Clearly Seligman identifies several therapeutic actions in the analytic process including [insight] but not limited to it. The holding environment can be seen as a form of [direct support] and the access to new interpersonal experiences would seem to require [introjection] that facilitates a shift in the patient's representation of the analyst. He explicitly refers to the process of [working through].*

According to Miller (2004), dynamic systems theory links the therapeutic relationship to the individual affective and physiological states of the patient and of the analyst. In so doing, it places the therapeutic action of psychoanalysis in the adaptive context of the formation and maintenance of the patient's attachment to the analyst and of the analyst's attachment to the patient. Changes in the emotional states of the patient and of the analyst are brought about through changes in the nature of their attachment to one another. *This focus on therapeutic action being brought about through attachment certainly points to the relationship as the agent of change, which in order to be lasting would require some form of internalization. The mutuality of Miller speaking in terms of the patient and the analyst's "attachment to each other" suggests it is the relationship that gets internalized, presumably through processes of [identification] and/or [introjection], though which is not specified.*

Smith (2004), writing about psychotherapy with childhood survivors of trauma, describes the one of the two primary mechanisms of therapeutic action as being catharsis, which he notes is underappreciated, and the other as internalization, by which he seems to be referring both to changes in the patient's self and object representations. He refers to the mastery of the traumatic emotions and the realignment of a distorted inner, representational world. *Thus, Smith is clearly emphasizing [catharsis], [introjection], and [identification].*

Ablon and Jones (2005) emphasize the interpersonal, interpretive interaction that both analyst and patient identify as repetitive and recurring. He describes the therapeutic action as located "in the recognition and understanding of these recurrent interactions by both analyst and patient." *Thus, Ablon and Jones are clearly emphasizing [insight] and [working through] in the repetition of the analyst's observations and comments about the meaning of the patient's associations.*

Andrade (2005) gives clinical examples that support the conviction that "therapeutic action arises from the reconstruction of the environment, in which the most distant and significant emotional experiences took place, causing a spontaneous blossoming of awareness out from this affective base, in which the analyst shows himself to be a different object to the original one." *In this view, Andrade is clearly emphasizing [insight] in that his emphasis is explicitly on awareness.*

Sugarman (2006) describes therapeutic action as engaging the patient in a process that promotes what he refers to as "insightfulness." He says, "Central to this technical approach is the importance of attending to the formal organization of patients' minds, as key mental structures and modes of mental functioning are manifested in the interaction between patient and analyst. This emphasis on facilitating a process of insightfulness, with its goal of helping patients achieve and maintain a stable ability to mentalize, wherein key mental functions, not just contents, are subjected to self-reflection and affective-cognitive self-knowledge, reverses figure and ground and the traditional emphasis on knowing just unconscious mental content."

He goes on to say, "A variety of benefits accrue from patients gaining insightfulness at an abstract-symbolic level of functioning. Self-other boundaries are strengthened as patients gain a cognitive-affective awareness that they have differentiated and conflicted minds that affect their behavior, and that others do also. Empathy improves with the realization that others' minds may be organized and function in different ways, or contain different feelings and beliefs. Interpersonal interactions are more easily understood and navigated by patients who can mentalize symbolically. Relationships feel safer as patients come to realize that others' actions are dictated by their mental functioning. Reality testing is facilitated, separation-individuation is promoted, and the primacy of secondary-process thinking is enhanced by symbolic mentalization. Finally, affect regulation is improved so that emotions can serve a signal function and not be experienced as overwhelming. *Sugarman is clearly speaking about [insight], but here we see a more complex process that involves other modes of therapeutic action as well. The idea that the patient internalizes the analyst's conceptualization of mind invokes [introjection as well as identification]. Repeated instances of [working through] must be part of the process that leads patients to know not only what is in their minds, but also and more importantly how their minds work; then to be able to see others from this vantage point. Given Sugarman's complex conceptualization, with its reliance on mechanisms of identification and introjection, it is not surprising that his recent thinking (Sugarman, 2012) has led to writing about the value of the analyst feeling freer about self-disclosure; when the analyst reveals something personal, the analyst becomes a more available object for internalization.*

Aisenstein (2007) describes the therapeutic action of psychoanalysis, compared to other talking cures, as indispensable because it alone aims at more than bringing relief from a symptom, but instead at aiding our patients to become, or to become again, the principal agents in their own history and thought. *Here she clearly speaks to [insight], but also to the patient becoming the "principal agents in their own history and thought." While she tends to oppose the idea that it is possible to identify distinct therapeutic actions, we can ask how someone develops this sense of agency and what is meant by it? In fact, I think this agency is a very complex aspect of psychic functioning that includes a sense of being active rather than passive, a sense of authenticity, of self-reflection, of self-awareness, and an appreciation for the unavoidable subjectivity of one's own perceptions; moreover, I doubt that these are the only elements involved. But this achievement is an outcome, not a mode of therapeutic action, and I suspect it is a far too complex and individualized achievement of the treatment to generalize about the specific modes of therapeutic action. Rather, I imagine that in any analysis, this achievement will involve various modes of action, in different proportions, at different times of the analysis. Rather than taking the position of Aisenstein, however, that it is not possible to identify specific modes of therapeutic action, I prefer the idea that it is impossible to generalize, such that it can only be done on a case-by-case basis.*

Hinshelwood (2007) in elaborating on Melanie Klein, comments that therapeutic action is the enhancement of the ego in its ability to contain its experience and tolerate its conflicts. *Here we see that the mechanisms of the therapeutic action(s) of the therapy are not specifically stated, but instead are put in terms of the goal of the treatment. At the end of the paper, however,*

Hinshelwood does say that the therapeutic action comes from "interpreting deep-going destruction of knowledge and self-knowledge in in the patient's mind, while the analyst's mind can (in good conditions) 'contain' the knowledge of this self-destructiveness." In other words, the emphasis is placed on [interpretation].

Kernberg (2007) raised the question, does interpretation leads to insight, or is it that the analysis of the therapeutic relationship leads to a new type of object relation? In answering his own question he says that he believes "the systematic interpretation of the transference is the major factor of therapeutic action specific to psychoanalysis, and that the unique type of personal relationship achieved in the context of a technically neutral relationship, centered on the analysis of the transference, permits the building up of a new, unique type of object relation that gradually becomes an additional, important therapeutic function as a consequence of the systematic transference analysis." *In other words, he says that it is both. Clearly there is an emphasis here on [interpretation], as he describes the systematic differentiating of past relationships from the present, via transference analysis. The mechanism(s) of building a new object relationship are less clear in this description, but presumably this would involve some form(s) of internalization on the part of the patient; given his focus on the therapeutic function of building up of a new object relationship, perhaps it would be best to think of the [identification] with and/or [introjection] of a new type of relationship with the analyst rather than the internalization of the analyst.*

Renik (2007) defines the therapeutic action of psychoanalysis as "the patient's increased capacity to make changes in his/her attitudes or behaviors in order to achieve greater well-being and satisfaction in life." He comments that most theoreticians agree with him, but notes how much they diverge in their view of how analytic technique will best accomplish this goal, and he says that the patient's experience of benefit is the best outcome measure. *Here Renik is not specifying the mode(s) of therapeutic action. Rather, he is specifying how to best measure if the analytic work is successful, opening up the analytic work to include any modes of therapeutic action that lead the patient to feel a "greater sense of well-being and satisfaction in life.*

Glick and Stern (2008) speak about an analyst hoping to be a new, healthy object for the patient, one that would be internalized and counter the pathogenic objects in the patient's mind. What they report, however, is that there was no protection from the patient's intensely conflictual transferences, including both his aggression and his hungers, and that therapeutic action involved the patient's experiencing and working through the various transference wishes and fears in the analytic interaction. *In this description clearly the emphasis is on [insight] or the recognition of transference distortions and [working through].*

Conclusions: While this is certainly not an all-inclusive review of the literature on the psychoanalytic treatment process and therapeutic action, the

views of a number of notable authors are represented and several patterns do emerge. First, there is no indication of a systematic trend favor-
ing particular modes of therapeutic action over time; in other words,
there does not seem to be any movement in the direction of a systematic
preference for a specific therapeutic action. Though it is not evident in the
manner in which I searched the literature, I do think it is reasonable to
assume that over time "the acceptance" of more diverse modes of therapeutic action has increased. Second, authors writing about psychoanalytic treatment tend to deemphasize catharsis in favor of direct support,
insight, identification, and introjection, perhaps due to a rejection of the
"pre-psychoanalytic" affect-trauma model. Where direct support is emphasized, it is in the service of facilitating the other, mutative forms of
therapeutic action. Where introjection and identification are part of the
therapeutic action, some authors stress autonomy and independence by
emphasizing the internalization of the analytic process and the working
alliance, whereas others explicitly include the internalization of personal
values and characteristics of the analyst. Concerning insight, there are
preferences for different conceptual targets of exploration and discovery,
not to be confused with different modes of therapeutic action; insight is
insight whether it concerns id, ego, superego, internal objects, true-self,
false-self, or any other concepts of mind for that matter. Working through
is rarely stressed, which raises concerns that psychoanalysts and analytic
psychotherapists have insufficiently appreciated the relevance of findings emphasized by behaviorists and more recently by neuroscientists,
which could inadvertently decrease the therapeutic impact of insights
gained through analytic treatment. It is not sufficient merely to see something in a new way, that insight has to be applied repeatedly in different
situations for real, lasting change to take place.

Overall, there can be little doubt that different authors emphasize
distinctly different albeit mutative modalities of therapeutic action. In
view of the fact that systematic approaches to psychoanalytic treatment
embrace different mechanisms of change, we cannot compare them without taking these fundamental differences into account. When describing a
particular analytic process, it is important to specify the preferred basic
mode(s) of therapeutic action. Perhaps it would be even better to think in
terms of there being various *analytic processes* than trying to reach a consensus about one analytic process, or to restrict an all-inclusive definition
of analytic process to being *mutative, transference based treatments*, and
leave out the techniques specific to different modes of therapeutic action.
In any event, it is important that psychoanalysts avoid getting caught up
in "straw man" distinctions, and in the narcissistic attachment to a particular point of view, as such divisions needlessly fragment and weaken the
voice of the profession.

SEVEN

Conclusions and Reflections

Before concluding, I want to comment on the implications of the six modes of therapeutic action for treatment recommendations, for the training of psychotherapists and psychoanalysts, and lastly for research about the talking cures. While my comments will be deceptively brief, the actualization of what follows is quite challenging, especially in today's world where there is a desire for everything to happen faster and cost less. Still, considering the explosion of the use of anti-depressants, considering that a 2012 Gallop Poll showed 87 percent of workers in the world are not happily engaged in their jobs, considering that the divorce rate in the United States is nearly half that of new marriages, to name but a few indicators, there is clearly a very significant need for ways to help people to lead more contented, fulfilling lives.

First, where treatment recommendations are concerned, it should be possible to achieve a better match between patient and treatment by assessing the fit between the basic modes of therapeutic action, comprehensive diagnoses, and a given patient's needs (Blatt, 1992; Gabbard and Weston, 2003). Rather than asking if a patient needs an analyst trained in object relations, modern structural theory, self-psychology, or relational psychoanalysis, rather than asking if a patient needs psychoanalysis, cognitive-behavioral psychotherapy, transactional analysis, hypnotherapy, behavior therapy, transference-focused therapy, emotionally focused therapy, mindfulness-based cognitive therapy, rational emotive therapy, dialectical behavior therapy, gestalt therapy, group psychotherapy, supportive psychotherapy, interpersonal therapy, or couples therapy, to name but a few, we would ask a more fundamental question: Which basic modes of psychotherapeutic action are the best fit given a particular patient's resources and needs? Once that question is answered, the next step would be to conceptualize upward and determine which systematic techniques of psychoanalysis or psychotherapy best emphasize that mixture of basic treatment modalities and will therefore fit the patient's needs and resources.

Of course, in order to be able to do assessments for psychotherapy in this systematic way, in this more individualized way, two basic requirements must be fulfilled. First, methods are required to assess which modes of therapeutic action are more likely to have success with which patients. I have attempted to address this issue in chapter 3 that gives all the examples of psychological testing. Second, the therapist has to know techniques of treatment that will emphasize the needed modes of therapeutic action or make the proper referrals: One size does not fit all! If the therapist is trained in all the basic modes of therapeutic action, it becomes possible to tailor the treatment to the individual patient, as can be seen in chapter 4 with the clinical example of individual treatment, where different modes of therapeutic action were relied on at different points of the treatment. But if treatment is going to be "manualized" it must be in this more individualized, comprehensive way. Alternately, if the therapist is trained to do a rote, manualized treatment that mechanically emphasizes and deemphasizes certain modes of therapeutic action, the patient must be referred to the "best fit" treatment accordingly.

Second, where professional training is concerned, the idea of conceptualizing upward from these basic modes of therapeutic action points to a common but potentially problematic approach to the education of psychoanalysts and psychotherapists. For the most part, we tend to teach the higher order, conceptual schools of psychoanalysis and psychotherapy, without first teaching the core, fundamental modes of therapeutic action basic to all of them. As a result, our teaching and supervisory methods can fail to convey a full appreciation of the basic, underlying mechanisms by which various systematic approaches to treatment produce their therapeutic effects. At best, students may not learn to put into words the ways in which their interventions are personalized to meet each patient's individual needs; at worst, they may recommend and conduct the same rote treatment for all patients, holding the view that certain modes of therapeutic action are inherently superior to others. Such blind allegiance to particular treatment methods, encouraged by an *esprit de corps* in the training experience, is a potential enemy of the patient's individual best interests and an obstruction to the scientific spirit of seeking the truth.

Third and last, where research is concerned, Fonagy (2001), in a commentary on papers by Lester Luborsky and Hans H. Strupp argues, "There is a need for refinement of the concepts and methods by which outcomes are evaluated in order to help psychoanalysis and psychotherapy become a more specific family of treatments for particular conditions." In psychotherapy and psychoanalytic research, by determining and trying to isolate the basic modes of therapeutic action in a given treatment, it should be possible to specify the independent variable(s), thereby refining our studies of treatment process and outcome. Surely this is a daunting task, but hopefully not impossible. Then the research could address the question of whether a treatment fail because it lacks therapeutic potential, or because its particular modes of therapeutic action are ineffective for a given patient?

In one striking example of such research, Blatt (1992) used a Rorschach Projective Test method for reevaluating the data from the Menninger Psychotherapy Research Project (a very sophisticated study comparing forty-two lives in treatment with either psychotherapy or psychoanalysis). He transformed one of the most carefully conducted outcome studies from a disappointing lack of findings to one with significant results. By re-diagnosing subjects according to developmental level of object relations, and reexamining the outcomes, he discovered that patients with a higher developmental level of object relations benefited significantly more from psychoanalysis, as compared to patients with lower developmental object relations, who benefited significantly more from face-to-face psychotherapy. Blatt defined the two independent variables, psychotherapy and psychoanalysis, according to their modes of therapeutic action, as follows: "In a broad and general sense psychotherapy may highlight more the interpersonal and relational dimensions and psychoanalysis more the interpretive dimensions." Thus, it is clearly true that more specific, refined definitions of therapeutic action, hence more refined independent variables, facilitate research when linked to more individualized, psychodynamic diagnoses.

Freud pointed the way. The various stages in the development of his thinking provide a way of understanding the mind and all of its treatments: six basic modalities of therapeutic action. It remains to explore and possibly delineate additional basic modes of therapeutic action; to refine an appreciation for which modalities are synergistic with and/or antagonistic to each other; to develop more research applications that link the basic modes of therapeutic action with diagnosis and treatment outcome; to classify and compare existing clinical theories systematically, including ones that are not psychoanalytic, for purposes of facilitating treatment recommendations; to incorporate such viewpoints into psychoanalytic curriculums; to develop methods for integrating more specific schemes of therapeutic action into the supervisory process; and to develop and deliver such applications of psychoanalysis to departments of psychiatry, psychology, social work, and all programs that train mental health professionals. Unquestionably much remains to be done.

References

Abend, S. M. (1979). Unconscious Fantasy and Theories of Cure. *Journal of the American Psychoanalytic Association*, 27:579-596.

Ablon, S. J. and Jones, E. E. (2005). On Analytic Process. *Journal of the American Psychoanalytic Association*, 53:541-568.

Aisenstein, M. (2007). On Therapeutic Action. *Psychoanaltic Quarterly*, 76:1443-1461.

Andrade, V. M. (2005). Affect and the Therapeutic Action of Psychoanalysis. *International Journal of Psycho-Analysis*, 86:677-697.

Aron, L. (2000). Self-Reflexivity and the Therapeutic Action of Psychoanalysis. *Psychoanalytic Psychology*, 17:667-689.

Bálint, M. (1969). Trauma and Object Relationship. *International Journal of Psycho-Analysis*, 50:429-435.

Bion, W. R. (1970). *Attention and Interpretation*, 1-130. London: Tavistock.

Bird, B. (1972). Notes on Transference: Universal Phenomenon and Hardest Part of Analysis. *Journal of the American Psychoanalytic Association*, 20:267-301.

Blatt, S. (1974). Levels of Object Representation in Anaclitic and Introjective Depression. *Psychoanalytic Study of the Child*, 29:107-157.

——— (1992). The Differential Effect of Psychotherapy and Psychoanalysis with Anaclitic and Introjective Patients: The Menninger Psychotherapy Research Project Revisited. *Journal of the American Psychoanalytic Association*, 40:691-724.

Blatt, S., and Behrends, R. (1987). Internalization, Separation-Individuation, and the Nature of Therapeutic Action. *International Journal of Psycho-Analysis*, 68:279-297.

Blum, H. (1981). Some Current and Recurrent Problems of Psychoanalytic Technique. *Journal of the American Psychoanalytic Association*, 29:47-68.

Brenner, C. (1982). The Concept of the Superego: A Reformulation. *Psychoanalytic Quarterly*, 51:501-525

Brenner, C. (1987). Working Through: 1914-1984. *Psychoanalytic Quarterly*, 56:88-108.

Brody, P. (1988). Couples Psychotherapy: A Psychodynamic Model. *Psychoanalytic Psychology*, 5:47-70.

Burrow, C. (2002). *The Complete Sonnets and Poems*. Oxford: Oxford University Press.

Caspary, A. C. (1993). Aspects of the Therapeutic Action in Child Analytic Treatment. *Psychoanalytic Psychology*, 10:207-220.

Chused, J. F. (1996). The Therapeutic Action of Psychoanalysis: Abstinence And Informative Experiences. *Journal of the American Psychoanalytic Association* 44:1047-1071.

Clyman, R. B. (1991). The Procedural Organization of Emotions: A Contribution From Cognitive Science to the Psychoanalytic Theory of Therapeutic Action. *Journal of the American Psychoanalytic Association*, 39(S):349-382.

Colarusso, C. A., and Nemiroff, R. A. (1981) *Adult Development: A New Dimension in Psychodynamic Theory and Practice*. New York: Plenum Press.

Dicks, H. (1967). *Marital Tensions*. New York: Basic Books.

Dollard, J., and Miller, N. E. (1950). *Personality and Psychotherapy*. New York: McGraw-Hill.

Eckardt, M. H. (2010). *The Embedded Self: An Integrated Psychodynamic and Systemic Perspective on Couples and Family Therapy*. New York: Routledge.

Ellman, J. P. (2000). The Mechanism of Action of Psychoanalytic Treatment. *Journal of the American Psychoanalytic Association*, 48:919-927.

Erb, W. (1883). *Handbook of Electro-therapeutics*, transl. by L. Putzel, New York.

Fenichel, O. (1939). *Problems of Psychoanalytic Technique*. New York: Psychoanalytic Quarterly Inc., 1941.

Fonagy, P. (2001). The Talking Cure in the Cross Fire of Empiricism—The Struggle for the Hearts and Minds of Psychoanalytic Clinicians. *Psychoanalytic Dialogues*, 11:647-658.

Frank, J. and Frank J. (1991) *Persuasion and Healing*. Baltimore: Johns Hopkins University Press.

Freud. S. (1887). Review of Weir Mitchell's Die Behandlung Gewisser Formen Von Neurasthenie Und Hysterie. *Standard Edition* 1: 36.

——— (1892). A Case of Successful Treatment by Hypnotism. *Standard Edition* 1:115-128.

——— (1893). Studies on Hysteria (Breuer and Freud). *Standard Edition* 2:3-17.

——— (1900). The Interpretation of Dreams. *Standard Edition* 4:Chapter 7.

——— (1923). The Ego and the Id. *Standard Edition* 19:50.

——— (1926). Inhibitions, Symptoms and Anxiety. *Standard Edition* 20:159-160.

——— (1938). An Outline of Psychoanalysis. *Standard Edition*. 23:172-182.

Gabbard, G., and Westen, D. (2003). Rethinking Therapeutic Action. *International Journal of Psycho-Analysis* 84:823-841.

Gedo, J. E. and Goldberg, A. (1973). *Models of the Mind: A Psychoanalytic Theory*. Chicago: University of Chicago Press.

Glick, R. A. and Stern, G. J. (2008). Writing about Clinical Theory and Psychoanalytic Process. *Journal of the American Psychoanalytic Association*, 56:1261-127.

Gray, P. (1982). "Developmental Lag" in the Evolution of Technique for Psychoanalysis of Neurotic Conflict. *Journal of the American Psychoanalytic Association*, 30:621-655.

——— (1987). On the Technique of Analysis of the Superego—An Introduction. *Psychoanalytic Quarterly*, 56:130-154.

——— (1990). The Nature of Therapeutic Action in Psychoanalysis. *Journal of the American Psychoanalytic Association* 38:1083-1096.

Greenberg, J. R. (1981). Prescription or Description: The Therapeutic Action of Psychoanalysis. *Contemporary Psychoanalysis* 17:239-257.

Greenberg, M. A., Wortman, C.B., and Stone, A.A. (1996). Emotional Expression and Physical Health: Revising Traumatic Memories or Fostering Self-Regulation? *Journal of Personality and Social Psychology* 71 (3): 588-602.

Hartmann, H. (1939). *Ego Psychology and the Problem of Adaptation*, 1-121. New York: International Universities Press, Inc.

Harwood, I. (2004). How the Psychoanalyst Working Primarily with one Person Can Make a Successful Couple Intervention: Or, Why Psychoanalysts Should not Back away from Working with Couples. *Psychoanalytic Inquiry*, 24:387-405.

Hinshelwood, R. D. (2007). The Kleinian Theory of Therapeutic Action. *Psychoanalytic Quarterly*, 76S:1479-1498.

Hoffer, A. (1993). Is Love in the Analytic Relationship "Real"? *Psychoanalytic Inquiry*, 13:343-356.

Hoffman, I. Z. (1994). Dialectical Thinking and Therapeutic Action in the Psychoanalytic Process. *Psychoanalytic Quarterly*, 63:187-218.

Horowitz, M. J. Marmar, C., Krupnick, J., Wilner, N., Kaltreider, N., and Wallerstein, R. (1984). *Personality Styles and Brief Psychotherapy*. New York: Basic Books.

Jacobson, J. G. (1993). Developmental Observation, Multiple Models of the Mind, and the Therapeutic Relationship in Psychoanalysis. *Psychoanalytic Quarterly*, 62:523-552.

Jacobs, T. J. (1990). The Corrective Emotional Experience — Its Place in Current Technique. *Psychoanalytic Inquiry* 10:433-454.

Jones, E. (1997). Modes of Therapeutic Action. *International Journal of Psycho-Analysis*, 78:1135-1150.

Kandel, E. (1999). Biology and the Future of Psychoanalysis. *American Journal of Psychiatry*, 156:505-524.

Kernberg, O. F. (1991). Aggression and Love in the Relationship of the Couple. *Journal of the American Psychoanalytic Association*, 39:45-70.

——— (2007). The Therapeutic Action of Psychoanalysis: Controversies and Challenges. *Psychoanalytic Quarterly*, 76S: 1689-1723.

Klein, M. (1946). Notes on Some Schizoid Mechanisms. In *The Writings of Melanie Klein*. Vol. 1. London: Hogarth, 1975.

——— (1952). On Observing the Behavior of Young Infants. In *The Writings of Melanie Klein*. Vol. 3. London: Hogarth, 1975.

Kohut, H. (1972). Thoughts on Narcissism and Narcissistic Rage. *Psychoanalytic Study of the Child*, 27:360-400.

Kohut, H. and Wolf, E.S. (1978). The Disorders of the Self and their Treatment: An Outline. *Int. J. Psycho-Anal.*, 59:413-425.

Kuhn, T. (2012). *The Structure of Scientific Revolutions*. 50th anniversary (4th ed.). Chicago: University of Chicago Press.

Levinson, D. J. (1978). *The Seasons of a Man's Life*. New York: Ballantine Books.

Livingston, M. (2007). Sustained Empathic Focus, Intersubjectivity and Intimacy in the Treatment of Couples. *International Journal of Psychoanalytic Self-Psychology*, 2:315-338.

Loewald, H. W. (1960). On the Therapeutic Action of Psycho-Analysis. *International Journal of Psycho-Analysis*, 41:16-33.

Luborsky, L. (2001). The Meaning of Empirically Supported Treatment Research for Psychoanalytic and Other Long-Term Therapies. *Psychoanalytic Dialogues*, 11:583-604.

Lucente, R.L. (1994). The Concept of Developmental Lines in Marital Therapy. *Psychoanalytic Social Work*, 2:57-75.

Malin, A. (1966). Projective Identification in the Therapeutic Process 1. *International Journal of Psycho-Analysis*, 47:26-31.

Meissner, W.W., S.J. (1979). Internalization and Object Relations. *J. Amer. Psychoanal. Assn.*, 27:345-360.

——— (1989). The Therapeutic Action of Psychoanalysis: Strachey Revisited. *Psychoanalytic Inquiry*, 9:140-159.

Mennenger, K. (1958). *Theory of Psychoanalytic Technique*. New York: Basic Books.

Michels, R. (2007). The Theory of Therapeutic Action. *Psychoanalytic. Quarterly*, 76S: 1725-1733.

Midgley, N. (2007). Anna Freud: The Hampstead War Nurseries and the role of the Direct Observation of Children for Psychoanalysis. *International Journal of Psycho-Analysis*, 88:939-959.

Miller, J. (1967) Concurrent Treatment of Marital Couples by One or Two Analysts. *American Journal of Psychoanalysis*, 27:135-139.

Miller, M. L. (2004). Dynamic Systems and the Therapeutic Action of the Analyst. *Psychoanalytic Psychology*, 21:54-69.

Modell, A. H. (1976). "The Holding Environment" and the Therapeutic Action of Psychoanalysis. *Journal of the American Psychoanalytic Association*, 24:285-307.

O'Connell, M. (2000). Subjective Reality, Objective Reality, Modes of Relatedness, and Therapeutic Action. *Psychoanalytic Quarterly*, 69: 677-710.

Rapaport, D., Gill, M., and Schafer, R. (1945). *Diagnostic Psychological Testing*. Chicago: Year Book Publishers.

Renik, O. (2007). Intersubjectivity, Therapeutic Action, and Analytic Technique. *Psychoanalytic Quarterly*, 76S:1547-1562.

Rosenblatt, A. D. (1987). Change in Psychotherapy. *Annual of Psychoanalysis*, 15:175-190.

Rustin, J. (1997). Infancy, Agency, and Intersubjectivity: A View of Therapeutic Action. *Psychoanalytic Dialogues*, 7:43-62.

Sandler, J. (1974). Psychological Conflict and the Structural Model: Some Clinical and Theoretical Implications. *International Journal of Psycho-Analysis*, 55:53-62.

Schwaber, E.A. (1990). Interpretation and the Therapeutic Action of Psychoanalysis. *Int. J. Psycho-Anal.*, 71:229-240.

Segraves, R. T. (1978). Conjoint Marital Therapy: A Cognitive Behavioral Model. *Archives of General Psychiatry*, 35:450-455.

Seligman, S. (2003). The Developmental Perspective in Relational Psychoanalysis. *Contemporary Psychoanalysis*, 39:477-508.

Sharpe, S. A. (2000). *The Ways We Love: A Developmental Approach to Treating Couples.* New York: Guilford.

Shimmerlik, S. M. (2008). The Implicit Domain in Couples and Couple Therapy. *Psychoanalytic Dialogues*, 18: 371-389.

Siegel, J. (2012). Denial, Dissociation and Emotional Memories in Couples Treatment. *Couple and Family Psychoanalysis*, 2:49-64.

Smith, J. (2004). Reexamining Psychotherapeutic Action through the Lens of Trauma. *Journal of the American Academy of Psychoanalysis & Dynamic Psychiatry*, 32:613-631.

Sorter, D. (1995). Therapeutic Action and Procedural Knowledge: A Case Study. *International Forum of Psycho-Analysis*, 4:65-70.

Stern, S. (2002). The Self as a Relational Structure. *Psychoanalytic Dialogues*, 12:693-714.

Stolorow, R. D. (1993). Chapter 3 - Thoughts on the Nature and Therapeutic Action of Psychoanalytic Interpretation. *Progress in Self Psychology*, 9:31-43.

Strachey, J. (1934). The Nature of the Therapeutic Action of Psycho-Analysis. *International Journal of Psycho-Analysis* 15:127-159.

Sugarman, A. (2006). Mentalization, Insightfulness and Therapeutic Action. *International Journal of Psycho-Analysis* 87:965-987.

———— (2012). The Reluctance to Self-Disclose: Reflexive or Reasoned? *The Psychoanalytic Quarterly, 81:627-655.*

Summers, F. (1997). An Object-Relations Model of the Therapeutic Action Of Psychoanalysis. *Contemporary Psychoanalysis*, 33:411-428.

———— (2001). What I Do With What You Give Me. *Psychoanalytic Psychology*, 18:635-655.

Thorndike, E. (1913). *Educational Psychology: The Psychology of Learning.* New York: Teachers College Press.

Waska, R. (2008). A Kleinian View of Psychoanalytic Couples Therapy: Part 1. *Psychoanalytic Psychotherapy*, 22:100-117.

Winnicott, D. W. (1958). Anxiety Associated with Insecurity. In *Through Paediatrics to Psycho-Analysis.* New York: Basic Books, 1975, page 99.

———— (1960). The Theory of the Parent-Infant Relationship. *Journal of Psycho-Analysis* 41:585-595.

Index

affects, psychoanalytic theory of signal or trauma, 19

catharsis. *See* therapeutic actions, six generic modes of

confidentiality, and clinical material, 30, 51

couples therapy, assessment and treatment: assessment of, 74; attachment as a basic human need, 67–68; distinguishing infatuation from mature adult love, 72–73; emotions' role in couples' problems, 69–70; how to conceptualize and recommend treatment, 74–75; human mind is always in conflict, 68–69; marriage and the challenge of numerous partnerships, 73–74; personality structure of each partner, 70–71; psychoanalytic contributions to, 65–66; psychoanalytic perspectives on being a couple, 71; statistics on marriage and divorce, 67; therapeutic action(s) and the treatment of couples, 75

deficit versus conflict, developmental and emotional, 17

diagnoses, clinical examples related to consideration of therapeutic action(s), 29; boy failing to thrive both in school and socially, 43–45; depressed and agitated adolescent boy, 31–32; inhibited lost young woman, 35–38; man with severe passivity and questionable intellect, 45–47; question of girl being neurotic or borderline, 39–42; refractory depression in middle

aged man, 33–35; young man with severe depression and despair, 47–50

direct support. *See* therapeutic actions, six generic modes of

Freud, Sigmund: approach to scientific discoveries, 11; brief history of his ideas about mental illness and treatment, 12; downsides of his methodology, 12; lost legacy of contributions, 2–3, 6; revolutionizes the psychology of the mind, 1–2; why revitalize his contributions, 5, 7, 8

grief reactions, pathological, 20

identification. *See* therapeutic actions, six generic modes of

insight. *See* therapeutic actions, six generic modes of

introjection. *See* therapeutic actions, the six generic modes

manualized psychotherapies, limitations of, viii–ix, 51

medications, as psychotherapeutic mode of action, 16

neurosciences, and working through, 25

post-traumatic stress disorder, 19

psychoanalysis, why the decline in its popularity, 3–4

psychotherapeutic action(s). *See* therapeutic action(s)

psychotherapist's personal therapy, reasons for, ix

About the Author

Lee Jaffe, PhD, is a training and supervising psychoanalyst at the San Diego Psychoanalytic Center, a clinical psychologist, and a clinical professor of psychiatry at the University of California San Diego, while maintaining a private practice of psychoanalysis and psychotherapy in La Jolla for the treatment of children, adolescents, adults, and couples. He has served on the editorial boards of the *Journal of American Psychoanalytic Association* and the *International Journal of Psychoanalysis*. He is a past president of the San Diego Psychoanalytic Center, the International Psychoanalytic Studies Organization, the Affiliate Council of the American Psychoanalytic Association, as well as a member on the boards of the American Psychoanalytic Association and the International Psychoanalytic Association. He has authored and co-authored journal articles in the areas of neuropharmacology, psychoanalysis, and psychological testing, and edited and annotated a book about how to assess patients for treatment. He has a passion for teaching the present-day, practical usefulness of Freud's ideas.

CPSIA information can be obtained at www.ICGtesting.com
Printed in the USA
BVOW03*1223110814

362142BV00003B/6/P